TimeExpress
PUBLISHING ANNEX

Books by David E, Oguzierem

Absolutely Unstoppable (2009)

Winning Political Struggles (2009)

Struggle Towards Empowerment (2010)

Outstanding Teachers Strategies (2012)

The Symbol of Change and Leadership(2013)

Politics, Development & Minorities in Nigeria (2016)

POLITICS, DEVELOPMENT & MINORITIES IN NIGERIA

a closer look at the developmental challenges and prospects in Etcheland

Designed and Printed by

TimeExpress Publishing Annex
1 Olodu Close, Off Olusegun Obasanjo
Road, By Unity Bank
Port Harcourt, Rivers State, Nigeria
07031200894, 08093816546, 08133034594
E-mail: timeexpressmedia@yahoo.com

Contents

Dedication

This book is dedicated to the following persons who made sacrifices for the liberation and development of the present day Etche society.

1. Chief J.H.E Nwuke
2. HRM Ochie ENB Opurum JP MFR (Onye-Ishi-Etche) Ochie of Etcheland
3. Chief Jonah Akor
4. Chief Samuel Achonwa
5. His Excellency, Chief Dr Dominic U. Anucha, fmr Deputy Governor of Old Rivers State
6. Prof. Reginald Nwankwoala

Acknowledgment

I gladly appreciate the encouragement and support of the following persons - His Eminence, Ochie E.N.B Opurum MFR (JP), Onye-Ishi-Etche; His Excellency, Eze Dr D.U Anucha, former Deputy Governor of Rivers State; Captain Sunday Nwankwo, Engr. Sam Nwankwo FNSE, President-General of Ogbako Etche Socio-Cultural Organization; Rt. Rev. Okechukwu P. Nwala, Bishop of Etche Anglican Communion; Prof Steve Amadi, Dean faculty of Engineering RSUST and Mr. Hillary Orjimor.

I am also indebted to the following personalities for their commitment to Next Etche Development Project, namely; Chief Allwell Onyesoh, Prof. Samuel N. Maduagwu, Prince Emma Anyanwu, Dr. Naboth Nwafor, HRH Eze Sir Ken Nwala JP, HRM Eze Samuel Amaechi, Chief Hon. Ephraim Nwuzi, Barr Monday Onyezonwu, , Air Vice Marshal Abel C. Peters, Prince Ogbonna Nwuke, Navy Cmdr Benson Onukwuru, High Chief Jerome Eke, Prof.

Steve Amadi, Dr. George Nwaeke, Chief Okey Amadi, Barr. Ikem Adiele, Mr. Silas Anyanwu, Hon. Chidi Oluo, Sir Isaiah Choko, Sir Adolphus .A. Amadi JP, Dr. Ikechi Nwogu, Chief Sir Dr H.U Anuonye, Mr. Charles Nwaonuala, Hon. Golden Ben Chioma, Hon. Nnamdi Okere, Chief Ambrose Nwuzi, Prof. Samuel Maduagwu, Dr. Naboth Nwafor, Barr. Monday Onyezonwu, Chief Dr. John C. Ihejrika, Chief Oliver Okeregwu, Mr. Sam A. Odum, Dr. Nnamdi Amadi, Chief Nwuke Anucha, Dr. Acho Nwokogba, Dr. Adol Nwaeke, Dr Paulinus Nwankwoala, Dr. Onyemachi Nwankwo, Chief Joseph Amaechi, Chief (Dr) Emmanuel Anele, Mr. Chidi Nwankwo, Chinyere Nwabeke, Barr. Gloria Akor, Dame Eunice Odum, Deacon Chibuzor Ogbonna, Chief Ambrose Nwuzi, Engr (Sir) Micah Nwogu, Chief Grant Ubani, Hon. Kelechi Nwogu, Hon. Nnanna Opurum, Hon. Tony Ejiogu, Hon. Gift Anyalabechi.

Finally, I express my sincere thanks to my family for their support and encouragement. To each and every-one, I am grateful, as your different contributions have made the writing of this book a rewarding experience.

Foreword

The present Nigerian political practice is founded on injustice and oppression. The majority ethnic groups absolutely dominate the minorities. The majority groups have deliberately continued marginalizing the minorities in the affairs of governance and developmental projects. In this timely book, David Oguzierem used the Etches as one case study among many of such ugly experiences.

It is the unfair and unjust treatment of minorities that is behind the crisis that has bedeviled our country today. Until we practice a system based on equity and justice, which will be favorable both to the majorities and minorities, we shall continue to grapple with crisis and tension.

What is the way forward? The way out is to design a developmental vision for the development of both the majority groups and minorities. Having a vision and setting its targets and the elements for its success are essential for a people to improve their performance, services and the efficiency of its response to future developments. This should be done with one goal in mind: that of serving the people and enhancing the status of the people, majorities and minorities inclusive. This is what we expect our political system to deliver.

Developmental progress is not a wish or a favour, or even a gesture of generosity on the part of the leaders, but it is a permanent, unconditional commitment by the leaders, the government and all the people, towards the minorities. This requires government controlled by the majority to strive to develop the society, within the framework of a clearly defined development strategy that must be carried out to the letter. If development is the government's top priority, it is the duty of the government to contribute to the success of the minorities. But this can be achieved only if every group and section of the country feels he or she is part of the on-going development process and has a stake in its success.

I believe promoting this kind of environment should top the priorities of any developmental vision and that providing the conditions leading to such an environment should be the ultimate priority of all the governments. It is not enough that a government provides these facilities for the present; it must ensure it provides them tomorrow, next year, in the next decade and in the future.

As already mentioned in this book, the younger generation is the future. They are the ones who will find the formula that will guarantee sustainable development process and stability both for themselves and for future generations.

The success of our younger generation is not a success for majorities alone, but a success for Nigerians everywhere, including the minorities. They are the prime target of any economic vision and every development effort. Any development vision must therefore aim at preparing the younger generation not only to keep pace with the new economy, but to also take the initiative and lead.

This book, ***Politics, Development and Minorities In Nigeria*** is timely. I recommend the book as a useful read on issues of politics, development, economy and the future of minority communities, especially the Etche Nation.

Prof. Steve Amadi
Dean, Faculty of Engineering, RSUST
Port Harcourt

PREFACE

If Etche people refuse to fight, they cannot rise. Until we rise, we cannot see greatness. Until we see greatness, we cannot be empowered. Let us fight to rise. Let us rise to win, and let us win to be great.

- David Oguzierem

PREFACE

THE MINORITIES PROJECT

Change does not roll in the wheels of inevitability, but comes through continuous struggle. And so we must straighten our backs and work for freedom. A man can't ride you unless your back is bent.

- Martin Luther King, Jnr

Political and economic marginalization, total neglect, deprivation and underdevelopment have been the common story of minority tribes since creation of Nigeria. The Nigerian state has, for over the years, established the 'us' vesus 'them' style of operation. Like the lion, the majority tribes would love to have their 'full' before allowing other lesser 'animals' to have a taste of the meal, that is, if it remains; otherwise they stay hungry. This has been the precedence over the years.

The majority tribes such as the Hausas, Yorubas, Ibos, Fulanis and the mini-majority such as the Igalas, Isokos, Benis, Urobos, Ibibios, Ijaws, Gbokosetc, have, for over the years, determined the management of affairs in Nigeria. On the other hand, minority ethnic nationalities such as Etches have been deprived of participation in national and state administration. This is very unfair and unjust to man and God.

This book will give us the opportunity to take a closer look at the world of minority tribes in Nigeria, especially, Etche people in Rivers State as a case study. We shall see their challenges and potential opportunities. This book will also be a guide to all neglected minority communities in Nigeria in finding solution to their communal problems and developmental challenges.

IS THERE HOPE?
I feel increasingly sad about the sorry state of affairs of the minorities in Nigeria, especially the Etches. Only a persistent sense of optimism about a brighter future lifts my sadness. I keep telling others and myself that all this despair, pessimism and fear are transient, and like a lonely cloud crossing a clear sky, it will soon disappear. What unites Etches largely surpasses their difference, but although the opposite is true for many other tribes, we still see those tribes heading toward unity and development.

This draws my attention about Etche discord which is not a good omen because under normal circumstances, we should form a single bloc in pursuit of The Etche Project. We will never be able to achieve this if trivia dominates our major concerns and negative attitude keep overwhelming the positive. Today's Etche crisis is not one of money, men, professionals, intellectuals, morale, land or resources. Thank God, we have these in average and are backed by beautiful opportunities.

The real crisis is rather one of leadership, management and perennial egotism. This is the kind of crisis that is bound to happen when lust for power prevails over granting people the love and care they deserve, and when the interests and destiny of one individual become more important than those of a whole people. This is also what happens when the interests of some groups and cliques benefiting from certain leaders are served instead of those of all the people.

When we look at the present Etche society, what we see cannot do us proud. The history of Etche people has been characterized by continuous struggle; struggle for survival, social justice, and political empowerment. For us as a people, the struggle has been very challenging. Someone has said, and I totally agree with him, that, "you are not a failure until you look for who to blame for it." I believe that our people have no one to blame for their state of affairs. In my opinion, we are not backward because we are from minority; I believe we are backward because we are not open to change. For instance, there are banks of scientific facts that point to the fact that Etche is a land of unlimited opportunities, endowed with vast natural resources (oil and gas) and varieties of food. I consider it, therefore, a paradox that thousands in this same blessed land still live far below the poverty line. We have refused to embrace change in a modern world. In a state of unlimited opportunities, yet we are too blind to see them. A blind man has no sense of value for the treasures around him.

It has been said, and I sense it is true, that development disrupts traditional, political, social and economical systems. In my motherland Etche nation, we have tried to prove the opposite. We, as a people, are adept at making only minor alterations and slight modifications. We steadfastly refuse to fundamental changes. We strive obsessively to fit modern ideas into traditional system. Where no traditional system exists, we refuse to be daunted and simply manufacture tradition. Our distinctive underdevelopment experience is a good example of primitive traditional practice and lack of credible leadership. I am referring here to the kind of action that suffocates credibility and leadership. There is a world of difference between a leadership that is based on love and respect, and one that is based on fear.

Credibility of leadership, can only be established through action and not words. I am referring here to the kind of action that distinguishes a leader who considers his people as his foremost asset, and not one who looks at them as a burden. Our vision as a people should be sharp, our goals should be clear, our resources are huge and should be harnessed, our will is strong so we should stand tall, ready to face the challenges ahead. Our mission is clear to become a national, pioneering hub of excellence and creativity in Rivers State nay Nigeria, and we are already striving to make it the Rivers premier food production area and oil and gas zone. We are confident we can reach this ambitious goals, thanks to our dedicated and enterprising spirit. This can be improved upon if government can provide the necessary infrastructure and environment. Etche will never settle for anything less than first place.

All that is needed in order to reach these goals is to show our people the right direction and nurture their potential for innovation, creativity, self-confidence, determination and leadership. Those who lead from the top of the pyramid end up leading only those on top, which is not how an exclusive development exercise should be carried out. Development is a common and concerted effort and requires common leadership, a true leader should select leaders from the ranks of his own people. Once he selects the right leaders, they will join him in forging ahead to develop sound acceptable master plan of progress.

Although failure is a great teacher, we cannot afford the time to learn from our failures. Human societies cannot be subjected to such a process. Because we are dealing with human beings, we must opt for a successful development experience and a scientific approach that can be applied in all Etche communities. We are growing in a sustainable way, entertaining ambitious development plans, moving quickly over several areas of development and learning all the time. I am as confident that all the elements needed in a distinguished Etche development process are available, as the ability of Etches to achieve their plans. Underdevelopment may have been our experience in the past, but there is solution. This book will explain how to move from this height to the way faward .

David .E. Oguzierem
Egwi Town, Etche, Rivers State
October, 2016

SECTION ONE

HISTORY & POLITICS

The only people who deserve freedom are those who are ready to fight for it every day.

-Maxim Gorky

CHAPTER ONE

WHERE ARE WE COMING FROM?

---◆---◆---

I am not interested in power for power's sake, but I'm interested in power that is moral, that is right and that is good

-Dr. Martin Luther King Jr.

---◆---◆---

Where did the Etches migrate from? What is the history of our lineage? Who are we as a people? Objective answers to these simple questions will provide a clue to our desired direction. On the other hand, wrong answers will lead us to the wrong direction.

In the book, **HISTORY OF ETCHE,** the authors wrote that there are several stories of Etche origin. These stories have been distilled into two main traditions.

Excerpt from the book reads; *the first tradition traces Etche origin to Igboland. It has Igbodo as the first permanent settlement of all Etche people. The second tradition traces Etche descent to the ancient Bini (now Benin) Kingdom and suggests that Igbo Anwhurinwhu is the cradle of all Etche people.*

THE BENIN VERSION(S)

The various stories which link Etche with Benin maintain that the people of Etche are of the Igala/Urbo stock. The stories suggest that the aborigines of Etche descended from Ekpeledo of Iduu and Oba in the ancient Benin Kingdom.

The high light of this version is that the people of Etche left the Benin Kingdom around the 7th century, and moved eastwards up to Aboh and veered off into the Orashi River and migrated through the Ndoni creek, settling for a brief while with Akalaka (the father of Ekpeye and Ogba) at the place now called Omoku. Then the Etche horde moved southwards along the Orashi River till they got to the Engenni River, which they crossed and moved eastwards to Abua. They moved from Abua to Ndele by land and then to Aluu through a track road known as Ozo Ahia Ekhe, to Eneka and eventually stopped at Igbo, the first Etche settlement.

Another variant of the Benin tradition tries to corroborate the first version by filling the gaps found in the first version. This variant suggests that the Etche horde moved out of the ancient Benin Kingdom during the reign of Oba Ewuare (c. 1140 - c. 1473) because of the Oba's tyrannies. The Ochichi (Ikwerre), Ogba and Ekpeye were said to be in the horde that left Benin during the said Oba's reign of terror.

This variant contends that the Ogba and Ekpeye flanked off at Ali Awoh (now Omoku), but the Ochichi (Ikwerre) group continued with a part of Etche to settle at Ozuzu, while the remaining column of Etche went on and settled down at Igbo at about the end of the 15ᵗʰ century thereby making Igbo the first permanent settlement of Etche.

When all is said and done, these stories of Etche's Benin pedigree cannot be waved aside. They have some merits as shall be shown presently. All over the lower Niger, particularly among the Ijaws, the Okirikas, Elem Kalabari, Ibani, Ikwerre, Ekpeye and Ogba the story of descent from Benin is a widespread motif. The Ijaws and by extension the Okirikas, Kalabari, Ibani explain it with the Mein tradition.

The Ikwerre and Ogbaa/Ekpeye groups plead the Akalaka legend to prove their common descent from Benin. Apart from the Mein tradition and Akalaka legends, there are also a number of artifacts of bronze objects discovered at widely spaced spots in the lower Delta. All these tend to suggest some early contact with Benin.

THE IGBO VERSION

The Igbo version is the second tradition of Etche origin. This version suggests that the people of Etche are of the Igbo stock. The main contention of this tradition is that Etche descended from Igbodo in the central Delta.

Igbodo is an Igbo community on the western side of the Niger. It came under the influence and political control of the Benin monarchy during the reign of Oba Ewuare (c. 1440 - c. 1473). Igbodo situates between Asaba and Agbor in the present Delta State of Nigeria. In point of distance, Igbodo and Agbor are less than 150 km from Benin city. They were like outposts to the Benin monarchy from the Northwest.

According to this tradition, the founder of Etche is Echie. His name, Echie was corrupted by the British colonizers and anglicized as Etche. Echie was the eldest member of the family that emigrated from Igbodo. He was thus the natural leader of the family and was called "Ochie". "Genie" simply means the guardian and leader of the group. This is the root of the title of the Etche traditional stool, Ochie of Echie. It is a title which dates back to the pre-historic time known as Mgbe Ndieche. The mother of Etche people is Nne Kolochie, the wife of Etche.

From the point of migration, members of the family that left together with Etche were Ohaji, Ohuhu, Ngwa, Ngor and Echie's younger sibling, Ochichi (the father of Ikwerre). It is believed that the emigration took place during the reign of Oba Esigie (c. 1517 - c. 1530) not Oba Ewuare. The movement was actuated by the immediate panic created by the advancing warriors from Idah, which headed to destroy the Benin monarchy in the 16th century AD. In that panic -stricken situation, the inhabitants of the various Igbo settlements on the fringe of Benin made haste to flee the area. They descended towards the Niger, crossed the river and moved eastward in different directions after leaving the Orlu area.

There is no denying the fact that there was a mass movement of people from the western Igbo settlements across the Niger in the 16th century A.D. This occurred in the wake of the extensive political disturbances, which resulted from the invasion of the Benin monarchy by an army from Idah. The crises occurred during the reign of Oba Esigie. Although the Benin kingdom did not collapse under the said attack, the war sparked off a chain of political upheavals in the 16th century Nigeria. It is not unlikely that the crises nay have created deep panic in western Igboland so much so that a horde of inhabitants of the settelements along this axis chose to flee.

According to this tradition, it was about that period of the mass movement of people from the western Igboland that the horde led by Ochie crossed the Niger and moved south easternward. As at the time the horde led by Ochie passed the Niger, the people of Onitsha had not arrived. The area of land presently inhibited by Onitsha was occupied by Oze people.

The story continues that the Ochie group maintained a south eastern movement through Awka, Orlu, Okigwe down to Owerri axis. It was not a straight and smooth journey. There was no destination in mind. It was an odyssey of a people in search of a safe and secure abode away from the endless turmoils of the central Delta and of the Benin Kingdom.

A variant of the Igbo tradition suggest that Ochie (Echie) came into Igbodo from Arochukwu, another version suggests that the place of entry was Umunoha. And yet another story suggests that he (Echie) came in through Oratta, crossed the Oguochie River and settled permanently at Igbodo.

This history shows that Etche people have a history of great lineage. We migrated from great kingdoms either ways. We are a people with rich traditional background considering our root.

OUR POLITICAL JOURNEY
Study on the political history of Etche people indicates that Etche Nation has once in the 60s produced a regional minister in the person of Chief J.H.E Nwuke from Okomoko in Etche Local Government Area. We have also been priviledged to produce a Deputy Governor of old Rivers State during the Second Republic in 1983 in the person of His Excellency, Chief Dr. Dominic Anucha from Omuma Local Government Area. To the best of facts and information available to me, these are the highest positions we have occupied as a people in River state and Nigeria till date.

Thirty-two years have come and gone since the Second Republic when Chief Dominic Anucha was elected the Deputy Governor of old Rivers State; we have not moved beyond this level. Worst still, we have not attained such position again, rather, we have been retrogressing.

For the purpose of emphasis, it is worthy to mention at this point that we share Rivers East Senatorial District together with two of our sister ethnic groups, namely: Okrikas and Ikwerres. Two Okirika sons have represented us at the Senate, twice. The incumbent senator, who is an Okrika son - Sen. Gorge Sekibo is taking his third shot in office. He re-contested for a third term with Hon. Andrew Uchendu-an Ikwerre son. Also, two Ikwerre sons have occupied the position at the Senate, twice, namely; Senators Obi Wali and John Mbata. It is sad to say that no Etche son has enjoyed the opportunity to represent Rivers East Senatorial District at the National Assembly. It is equally worthy to note that no Etche son has been appointed as Secretary to Rivers State Government. Our law-makers have never been elected to serve as the Speaker of Rivers State House of Assembly.

We have never been considered for the position of the Governor of Rivers State. None of our sons or daughters has been considered for appointment as a Minister of the Federal Republic or Ambassador of Nigeria, nor has ever risen to the position of Federal Permanent Secretary. We have never held the position of the Board chairman of a Federal Parastatal or the likes.

More importantly none have served as the chairman of the ruling political party, either in the state or federal. Now the bigger one: no Etche man has ever been a party presidential flagbearer of any political party in Nigeria. The common question is: why have we not risen to these positions? The answer is very simple. Disunity! It is disunity that has led to loss of political identity, but then there is also the issue of minority.

This fact may be very bitter. But the truth is, we are a people that have not adequately formulated a political identity in Nigeria. Consequently we are not considered as a force to be reckoned with and so can easily be taken for a ride. Since no one cares to ask questions, it therefore seem that we lack the will to challenge the status quo, and muscle a change. We have not formidable and resolute in our political approach.

In this chapter, we will be exploring the past and present attempt to fashion political identity for Etche people. I will also attempt to act as a gadfly, a catalyst, to provoke discussion and dialogue on how best to reclaim our lost political identity.

ETCHE NATION MODERN POLITICAL EVOLUTION

The father and leader of modern Etche political evolution is late Chief J.H.E Nwuke. He joined partisan politics in 1944. The National Council of Nigeria and the Cameroons (NCNC) was formed on August 26, 1944, immediately after the Second World War. The formation and emergence of the NCNC was significant for Etche political history. It was the first political party to gain a foothold in Etche land. Late Chief J.H.E. Nwuke was a close ally of late Dr. Nnamdi Azikiwe one of the founders of NCNC.

From the time Chief Nwuke joined the NCNC, the political wave changed in Etche. Chief Robert Nwuche of Eberi in Omuma also joined the NCNC at about this time and tagged along Chief Nwuke and Chief Aguma. Chief Robert Nwuche eventually became the first Vice Chairman of Etche County when it was created in 1952. Late Chief S.O Achonwa was the first Chairman. When the County Council was divided into three regions, namely; East, West and North, Etche belonged to the Eastern Region. The Eastern Region was administered from Enugu between 1946 and 1967. Etche formed an integral part of Ikwerre/Etche and Ahoada Federal Council. The Federal council was composed by the federating clan councils. The headquarters of Ahoada, Ikwerre / Etche federal council was Ahoada.

The Ikwerre/Etche/Ahoada Federal Council was chaired by an Etche son, Chief J.H.E. Nwuke. Under the Federal Council, Etche was shared into three parts. Omuma belonged to Aba Division, Ozuzu to Owerri Division and the other parts of Etche fell to Degema Division

Conscious of the advantage inherent in keeping all the parts of Etche together, Etche political elite of the time had series of talks and lobbies at Asa, Degema and Port Harcourt for all of Etche to be reassembled into a single administrative unit. Chief M.E. Nwankwo from Omuma tenaciously fought for the integration of Omuma with Etche.

Based on the recommendation of the Ackwright Commission, Omuma area of Etche was brought back to Etche mainland and the Ikwerre/Etche Amalgamated County Council broke up in 1952. Etche County Council was thus established with its headquarters at Eberi. The headquarters was finally moved to Umuola (Obibi) in 1964, and was finally moved to Okehi for reason of centrality.

The creation of Etche County Council marked the first major revolution of political autonomy by the people since 1906, the year that Etche was placed under the Eastern province. Immediately after the federal election of 1964, Chief J.HE. Nwuke was elected to the Eastern Regional Assembly from where he got appointed as a Regional Minister into the Eastern Regional Executive Council. Chief Jonah Akor was elected into the Federal House of Representative to represent the defunct Ahoada North/East Federal Constituency. Both Chief Nwuke and Chief Akor were of the NCNC.

The Nigeria/Biafra Civil War broke out in 1967. The war left Etche blighted. First, Etche was occupied by Biafran insurgents until they were dislodged and driven away by the federal troops. During the war, countless number of Etche people perished. The Chokocho-Umuanyagu-Okomoko Bridge, the Umuechem-Egwi and Umaturu - Akpoku Bridges were blown up by the Biafran soldiers to hinder the federal troops from gaining access to the lgbo heartland. The people of Etche were displaced, dislocated and dragged back in terms of progress. The cost of the war in Etche was enormous.

The lot of Etche in the years after the civil war became bitter. There were no accessible roads and bridges to enhance movement of people and goods in and out of Etche. Life in the area became localized as people engaged in farming to meet subsistence needs. Economic activities nose-dived; poverty proliferated and the people's living standard diminished. Since the military were still in power, no partisan activities went on. Worst still, Chief J H E Nwuke, the pathfinder of Etche politics, perished with the civil war. He was said to have been killed by a stray bullet. The effort of people of Etche to reintegrate into Rivers State was checkmated by the Riverine people. Riverine people of Rivers State were slow to accept and accommodate the people of Etche (and other upland Rivers) as part and parcel of Rivers State. They disregarded the fact that Etche County Council was one of the 17 county councils that constituted Rivers State since 1967. Indeed, it took the great efforts of Eze E.N.B. Opurum to get Etche fully integrated into Rivers State after the war. Eze E.N.B. Opurum was then the Commissioner of Rural Development and Co-operative.

He was the first Etche person to be made commissioner in Rivers State.

However, the post-war military administration in Rivers State under Commander Alfred Diete Spiff recognized and respected Etche political autonomy., When Alfred Diete-Spiff created Divisional Councils, Etche was constituted into a separate Divisional Council (1973-1975). That was a fresh stamp of recognition on the autonomy of Etche which was won in 1952. Regrettably, the Divisional Council arrangement did not last long before it fizzled out.

In 1976, the Federal Military Government of Nigeria carried out a nation-wide local government reform. Consequently, the Divisional councils in Rivers State were reconstituted into Local Government Areas. At this time, Colonel Zamani Lekwot had become the Military Administrator of Rivers State. He looked back into the arrangement in 1950 and once again put Ikwerre and Etche together to form Ikwerre/Etche local Government Area (KELGA), with Isiokpo as the headquarters.

The creation of KELGA in 1976 was a major turning point in the political history of Etche. From that development, Etche people lost the political autonomy they attained in 1952.

From 1976, May 3 to 1989, darkness fell in Etche. Etche people suffered acute political marginalization. They were oppressed, traumatized, and deprived. Virtually all benefits meant for KELGA eluded Etche.

However Etche opinion leaders did clamour relentlessly for better treatment from successive Rivers State governments. Sadly though, all their complaints fell on deaf ears. The suffering and deprivations refused to ease. Etche had no one in the government, state or federal level. There was no one to advocate for her cause in the corridors of power. The sad lot of Etche persisted until the Transition to Civil Rule in 1979.

The Transition to Civil Rule started in earnest in 1978. The Federal Military Government convened the Constituent Assembly where the 1979 Constitution was debated and packaged. Etche was not represented at the Constituent Assembly because the single chance for KELGA was, as usual, filled by Ikwerre.

Subsequently, the Federal Military Government registered five political parties: the National Party of Nigeria (NPN), Nigerian Peoples Party (NPP), Unity Party of Nigeria (UPN), Great Nigerian People Party (GNPP) and the People's Redemption Party (PRP). The people of Etche embraced the NPP more than the other parties.

From the general elections of 1979, Etche elected her compatriots to represent her at the state and federal levels of government. Thus, late Dr. E. O. Nwala of NPP defeated Chief Nwanoruo M. Okere of NPN to represent Etche Federal constituency in the Federal House of Representatives, Lagos. At the state legislature, Dr. D.U

Anucha of NPN was elected to represent Etche Constituency I and Barrister S. O. Nwogu of NPP was elected to represent Etche constituency ll.

The NPN won the presidential election, though under a very controversial circumstance and formed the federal government, led by Aihaji Shehu Shagari. In Rivers State, Late Chief Melford Okilo of NPN won the gubernational election impressively. He became the first executive governor of Rivers State, with late Dr. Frank Eke as his Deputy.

The victory of the NPN was a great blessing to Etche. Late Chief Nwanorue M. Okere was appointed Commissioner for Commerce and Industry and later redeployed to the Ministry of Agriculture and National Resources. He thus became the second Etche son to be appointed Commissioner in Rivers State. Dr. D. U. Anucha was also elected the Deputy Speaker of Rivers State House of Assembly while Barrister S.O. Nwogu of NPP became the Deputy Minority leader in the same Assembly. Also Mr. Reginald Nwabeke was appointed Commissioner for Electricity and Water Supply (1979- 83).

Chief James Nweke functioned as the Chairman of Omuma Urban Council between 1979 and 1983 and Chief T. O. S. Anaele served as the Chairman Etche District Council 1981/82.

Earlier, Chief L. A. N. D. Nwankwo had served as the Chairman of KELGA from 1980-81, being the first Etche to hold the position of a Chairman of the Council since 1976 when it was created. Later in 1983, Chief Ben Chioma also had a stint as caretaker Chairman of KELGA.

From October 1979 - December 31, 1983, Etche basked in the sunshine of political fortune and glory. For instance, Chief D. U. Anucha became the Deputy Speaker of the Rivers State House of Assembly. The people's burden lessened for a while. The Second Republic was terminated on December 31, 1983. NPN swept the polls at all levels of government and got re-elected almost everywhere in the federation. In Rivers State, Chief Melford Okilo was returned as the Governor. This time, he picked an Etche son, Hon. D. U. Anucha as the running mate.

His Excellency, Hon. D. U. Anucha thus became the Deputy Governor of Rivers State. Barrister S.O. Nwogu had earlier defected to NPN at the Rivers State House of Assembly. Regrettably, these Etche sons were in power for only a short period before the military ousted the civilians from power on December 31st, 1983.

The duo of Major General Muhammadu Buhari and Brigadier Tunde ldiagbon ousted the civilians from power for alleged wide spread electoral malpractice, corruption, maladministration and economic chaos in the country. The 1979 Constitution was suspended and all the democratic structures were disposed off. The "shakers and movers" of the Second Republic were clamped into detention.

From January 1, 1984, darkness fell again in Etche. The events that followed left no one in doubt that the people of Etche had gone back to the pre-1979 era. According to the foremost scholar, late Professor R. N.P. Nwankwoala in his memoir, My Stewardship: *"the period was to Etche a perfect definition of hell on earth"*.

The people of Etche passed through another period of excruciating experience. They were deprived, oppressed and traumatized. There was anguish. Etche was on the margin. Actuated by anguish, the people of Etche began to explore every avenue to lift themselves out of their predicament. They became restless in their demand for the creation of Etche Local Government Council.

Hence in April 23, 1988, when late Dr. R. N P. Nwankwoala (as he then was) was elected to represent Etche Federal Constituency in the 1988/89 Constituent Assembly, his only obsession was how to get a local government council for the people of Etche.

Several petitions and memoranda were sent to the military authorities by the Ogbako Etche leadership under Chief (Barrister) S.O. Nwogu. Several useful contacts were also made; all in a bid to get a local government council for Etche. But the L.G.A. would not come. On December 12, 1988, late Dr. (later Professor) R.N.P. Nwankwoala moved an epic motion at the Constituent Assembly, advocating the creation of new

Local Government Councils in Nigeria based on Federal Constituencies.

The effect of the motion was enormous and provided the basis for the creation of additional 145 Local Government Councils in Nigeria by Gen. Ibrahim Babangida in 1989. Thus, on May 3, 1989 when Gen. Ibrahim Banbangida, in a nation-wide broadcast, announced 145 new Local Government Councils based on Federal constituencies, Etche Local Government council was named. There was wide jubilation and celebration all over Etche. It was like a day of independence. A new page was opened in the political history of Etche.

In 1995, Gen. Abacha convoked a Constitutional Conference in Abuja headed by Hon. Justice Adolphus Karibi-Whyte. Representation to the conference was based on senatorial zones. Accordingly, Chief (Dr.) D.U. Anucha, an illustrous son of Etche, was elected to represent the Rivers East Senatorial Zone. Another Etche son, late Mr. Alloys Nweke, who later represented Etche Constituency ll at the Rivers State House of Assembly, (1999 -2003), served as the Press Secretary to Hon. Justice Karibi-Whyte at Abuja throughout the period of the Constitutional Conference.

During the Constitutional Conference, the issue of creating more local government councils became a subject of serious discussion. Etche made representation to the Committee on local govornment creation, which was headed by Sir Dr. Peter Odili (Who later became the

Executive Governor of Rivers State). Etche demanded additional Local Government Areas to wit: Omuma and Otamiri LGAs. The Constitutional conference concluded its assignment and submitted its recommendation to the Provisional Ruling Council (PRC)

On December 5, 1996, the military administration of late Gen Sani Abach promulgated decree for the creation of more Local Government Councils in Nigeria and Omuma LGA was named. The creation of Omuma LGA was another watershed in the epic struggle of Etche people for political autonomy and recognition of the plight of Etche people, especially in the area of movement that is made difficult by its geographical terrain.

Etche thereby became composed of two LGAs: Etche and Omuma. The headquarters of Omuma is Eberi. Both LGA's make up the Etche Federal Constituency, with three state constituencies. Etche LGA has two state constituencies while Omuma LGA has one state constituency. Etche and Omuma still have one Federal Constituency.

CHAPTER TWO

THE NEW VISION

If a man hasn't discovered something that he will die for, he isn't fit to live.

-Dr. Martin Luther King Jr

I have always had this special feeling and concern about minority societies in majority dominated groups in our Nigerian nation especially as it affects Etche people. As early as I can remember, I have been fascinated by its peculiarity, inspired and spurred by its almost boundless human and material resources. In the years, as I grew up, this special feeling has crystallized into indissoluble commitment to my people; a people sometimes good and rarely excellent; sometimes bad and often downright failures.

This self-confidence, to the untutored, takes on the aspect of vaulting insensitivity. I have, in particular, been moved always by the poverty, squalor, ignorance, sickness and weakness of its common folk. I have, with the common folk, wept in anguish when successive governments and leaders exploit them mercilessly, dash their hopes on the rock for personal interest and self-aggrandizement, and fed them the diet of unfulfilled promises.

I have had a love/hate relationship with Etche. When I love, it is with all the consuming passion of mother's love for her retarded offspring and when I have appeared to hate, it has been with the hatred of a rejected suitor. From time to time, I frown at what I see happen in Etche. This has been, without exception, a lover's quarrel: volatile and very transient. My father is from Egwi in Etche Local Government Area; my beloved mother hails from Eberi, in Omuma Local Government Area. My paternal grandparents are both from Etche local government area. My maternal grandparents come from Etche and Omuma Local Government Areas respectively. I was also reliably told that my great grand parents are indigenes of Etche. Therefore, I regard myself as a full-blooded son of Etche of Niger Delta.

Moreover, I grew up in my beloved rural village-Egwi Etche. I had my primary school education at Egwi Primary School. My secondary education was at County Grammar School, Ikwerre/Etche; the only outside educational influence that I had was my university education at Rivers State University of Science and Technology and later University of Port Harcourt. I was raised on Etche soil. I know the pain and gain of the people. In my lonely moments, I reflect on the pendulum swing of Etche political emotions: day before yesterday - a fair government, yesterday - a bad political leadership; today -dialogue and tomorrow, very uncertain. From this,

I learnt that Etche people were beset with 'political blindness' and 'political identity' crises. Who are we? Where are we? Where are we going to? What shall we find there? And what shall we do with what we find there? These are very simple questions. Yet they are crucial to our existence, vital to our well being as a people and pertinent to The Next Etche Development Project(NEDEP).

I have reflected on all these. I have emerged from this background strengthened in my faith in Etche, sustained by an obsessive jealously for her image, and driven by unalloyed concern for the well being of her people. I feel proud that I am from Etche, for no ethnic nationality can match the hope which this beloved land of ours gives to the suffering and brutalized, wherever, and in whatever circumstance he finds himself in this country questionable country called Nigeria. But I think something very vital is lacking. What is lacking is the positive vision which can inspire and guide an eager people into the future.

From the lowest depths to the highest mountain tops, let me proclaim this vision of a new Etche and Niger Delta minorities.

I see an Etche and in which we all believe in the sanctity of human life and the dignity of the human person, an Etche where the willful and wanton destruction of human life is not only an abominable sin, but also a grave crime, an Etche where every individual counts, and no one is taken for granted; an Etche that upholds the dignity of man.

I see an Etche which places a high premium on patriotism and Etche people who have faith and devotion to the fatherland; an Etche where every indigene is prepared to work for the land and to stand up for her. I see an Etche where every indigene knows and demands his civil and political rights in Nigeria, recognizes the rights of his fellow Etcheman and is prepared to defend them when necessary and an Etche where we all stand up for our rights and assist others to secure their rights.

I see an Etche where sovereignty and power belong to the people; an Etche where the leader is servant and the ruled, master; an Etche where leaders strive to satisfy the people at all times.

I see an Etche where those who exercise power are accountable to the people; an Etche where leaders accept responsibility for inefficiency and bad advice.

I see an Etche that is very developed and peaceful, where the poor are taken care of, children are given education, and its youths empowered.

I see an Etche whose sons vie for and are appointed to the positions of minister, senator, ambassador, governor, vice president, chairman of boards, federal parmanent secretaries and someday, President of the Federal Republic Nigeria.

I see an Etche that has reclaimed its dreams and an Etche that has rediscovered her destiny.

OUR DESTINY IS IN OUR HANDS

The general population of Etche people is crippled by lack of hope; our people cannot imagine change and have therefore remained passive. Let passive nature not be mistaken for docility, for this land belongs not only to our often misguided political elite, but rather to all its indigenes. We must always remember that whenever a people grow weary of any system, they can always exercise their constitutional rights of orientating it, or should the situation demand, exercise their revolutionary right, to vote it out.

As we look with anguish at our beloved Etche, we find that she suffers gravely of two main diseases: lack of political empoerment and economic decline.

What I propose, and have been proposing in the search for a new understanding is a form of symbiosis during which we diffuse and contain our sicknesses until a new Etche emerges with virile anti-bodies to destroy the afore-mentoned diseases. In the search for political empowerment, let us be pragmatic and participatory. To halt our economic decline, let us install with urgency an era of manpower building and planned production with ever-increasing targets for each commodity and services.

If the anticipated new dispensation is to have any change of success, we must jointly march forward into the future determined to lower the level of political distrust; ensure that power is something to be shared rather than hoarded; increase with urgency the level of tolerable poverty in our society, and understand that too much change in too little time is as bad as too little change in too much time.

When we are committed to these, let us then proceed with courage to redesign a new majority which will not divide our beloved Etche land into right and wrong. What the new situation calls for, under the new understanding, is a division into right and left. This will usher in balance and stability and will be a second foundation for empowerment.

The prize is one of epic proportions and failure is not an option. To ensure success, we have to join the race and win. After all, no one ever remembers who came second - not even the second man to climb Everest Mountain or walk on the moon!

A people's development, however, does not happen overnight or by accident. Nor does the development of a nation ever stop once the process has begun.

Nation building is the result of intense efforts at building a community and homeland; a phenomenal task not undertaken lightly, but shouldered by a people's government, its public and private sectors, and its

They must all be willing to respond to the rapidly changing conditions that ricochet around the world at breakneck speed.

In order to lay solid foundations for the Etche future, we must build upon the achievements forged by our founding fathers - achievements that must not stop with our generation, but must continue and be perpetuated by future generations. History shows no mercy for weaklings. Late Chief J.H.E Nwuke; His Eminence, Eze E.N.B Opurum; His Excellency, Eze Dr. Dominic Anucha, Chief Jona Nwankwo and our beloved late and living leaders, never waited for history to record their feats; they were proactive in making history themselves and in doing so, set the benchmark for us to follow.

'Progression' and regression

In today's fast-paced world, if you are not leading, you will be left behind. If you fall behind, it is likely that someone less capable, less creative and less prepared than you will take your place. Although this can happen very quickly, the race is also one of endurance. Should you stumble once or twice, do not worry, you can learn valuable lessons from falling occasionally and will be unlikely to repeat the same mistakes. Failure is not falling to the ground; it is remaining there once you have fallen and the greatest failure is when you decide not to stand up again.

Etche leaders should fully understand that if our ethnic nationality lags behind others politically and economically, it will be left behind. They should also know that large-scale development will not only improve Etche's physical infrastructure, but eliminate unemployment, ignorance, poverty and illness.

When nations fail to develop, they become vulnerable to a collapse in security and stability, and lose the foundations on which their prosperity was built. They also risk being subjugated to tyranny and prejudice, and after a few years of recession, lose most of the benefits, status and respect they had acquired over several decades of development.

When you face a challenge that demands a solution or a decision, you have two choices - you can either emulate the example set by others or use your own creativity and intelligence to formulate a new idea. This applies equally to the development of our ethnic nationality. Many brilliant ideas have circulated the state and various groups have copied the concepts, so much that these once inspired creations often become hackneyed. However, 'second-hand' ideas are not for us here in Etche. We should rather lead than follow.

At the root of any new project is an idea and if we cannot find a fresh concept for a project, we will not implement it because it will fall short of what we have come to expect. We believe that the shortest way to the bright future we seek lies in a creative and pioneering approach.

I believe the task of our leaders needs to include the selection of an appropriate number of suitably qualified Etche manpower, with an eye to succession. This does not apply only to traditional institutions, but in other areas as well, especially politics, because it is a leader's duty to develop the leadership skills of those he believes are suitable. And when the time comes, these people can transfer their knowledge to the next generation.

While this happens most of the time, there are unfortunate exceptions. Some leaders are not interested in - or will not tolerate - the existence of another person as qualified and skilled as they are, out of fear of competition or of losing their position. Although this is understandable to a degree, I disagree with such leaders, because a true leader should realize he cannot be everywhere all the time and implement all his tasks at once. He must learn to delegate. When a leader fails to delegate, he will find himself embroiled in so much detail that it will eventually overwhelm and distract him from his primary task (developing the business of the office and finding innovative solutions to its problems) to such an extent that he will eventually lose sight of the bigger picture. It should also be known that success without a successor is failure. So good leaders should not only learn to carry others along but should also inspire and reproduce themselves in others.

But what exactly is the bigger picture?
The bigger picture is one of survival - life's driving force and the reason why all creatures spend each day trying to catch their prey or escape their hunters. Survival cannot be achieved by wishful thinking. Continued growth requires huge effort, complete attention and being consistently alert to potential dangers.

If our sole goal is to attain the level others have reached, then we are setting our target too low. We must take matters into our own hands. Do not fool yourselves into believing that we are moving forward when we are only keeping up with general trends, while the real opportunities are slipping away.

We must take the lead and be proactive in forging our own destiny. The future will bring daunting, unforseen challenges and we must be ready to face anything.

God gave his believers sight, vision and perception, to understand their environment and the consequences of their actions, both today and tomorrow. God's glory is evident in everything. You see it in the contrast between people; you find it in the strong and the weak, the rich and the poor, the leader and the follower.

I end this chapter with the famous Igbo proverb: 'Until lions have their own historians, tales of the hunt shall always gorify the hunter".

CHAPTER THREE

OIL & GAS
POLITICS IN ETCHE

―――――――――――◆―――――――――◆―――――――――

*Oil and gas virtually monopolize our
attention but these are resources that will
be taken out and finished in a few years.
What will remain to feed us, our children,
and their grand children are the other
resources of the land, rivers, seas and forests
which have endured from the over ten thousand
years life of the present Niger Delta. Our
attention, therefore, must extend beyond the
control of revenue from oil and gas,
to the preservation of the other
resources (of the environment) which are
the key to sustainable development.*

―Professor E.J. Alagoa

―――――――――――◆―――――――――◆―――――――――

SPDC, the largest multi-national oil company (MNOC) operating in Nigeria, had at 31 December 2006, 391 flow stations, and 6,200 pipelines and flow lines in 3,000 square kilometers in a variety of extreme habitats, including humid swamp Crests, mangrove swamps, seasonally flooded forests and the sea, SPDC is said to have formulated policies whereby all its activities are planned and executed to minimize environmental degradation, and the company recognizes [3] gap between its intentions and its current performance. The company is further said to be working hard to renew aging facilities, reduce the number of oil spills and the amount of gas that is flared.

Investigation reveals that these statements are merely on paper. In reality, SPDC and other MNOCs continue to devastate the environment and plunder the resources of Niger Delta people. Even where they enter into a

Memorandum of Understanding (MoU) with the host communities, SPDC, and indeed, the other MNOCs never keep to the terms. Investigations show that 86.5 percent of the conflicts between MNOCs and their host communities result from the non-adherence of MNOCs to the terms and conditions of the MoUs.

Several International declarations has been made since 1958 on the need to save the environment from destruction, clean up the polluted environment and develop host communities, yet the oil and gas companies continue with their activities that daily threaten the Niger Delta people. Our records show that there were 1,350 oil wells/flow stations as at 31 December 2006 and out of this number, 1,154, wells, representing 95 percent were located in the Niger Delta Region (Etekpe, A: 2007,). Etche remains the second largest producer of oil and gas with over 250 Oil-Wells located in its territories, which includes Umuechem, Egwi, Odagwa, Igbo, Umuebule, Okoroagu etc.

Realistically, saving our environment cannot be achieved by mere persuasion of the MNOCs, but by effective mobilization of researchers with appropriate empowerment/resources monitor the environment and carry-out remedial action to pre-empt disasters, people's apprehension that persuasion or dialogue has failed is based on history. The history is that, whereas with palm oil, the Niger Delta communities negotiated the terms directly with the Western supper cargoes, in the case of crude oil and gas, these communities can only stand on the side lines and receive the full impact of environmental degradation. The people have no input as to how the MNOCs should be environment-and-host-community friendly. This encompasses faithful adherence to MoUs and how victims of environmental disasters can be promptly and adequately compensated.

For example, the Umuechem Crisis of 1990, points to the fact that frustrations resulting from degradation of the environment and the increasing sense of powerlessness within the Nigerian political system propelled the violent conflicts. Besides, MNOCs apply "divide-and-rule" tactics that instigate "intra-and-inter" communal conflicts, in the process of oil exploration and exploitation.

The Federal Government, on its part, has not done much to protect the host communities. Instead, it partners with MNOCs to enact obnoxious laws that rather protect every other stakeholder in the industry except the oil producing communities. Thus, there is a lingering feeling that the Federal Government remains essentially external to the Niger Delta. Even the State Governments remain as external agents and display a care free attitude to the problems of local Communities. The frustrations/problems have sprouted new radical movements from the period of Isaac Adaka Boro's declaration of a Niger Delta Republic in 1966 to the

Umuechem massacre and Ogoni debacle in the 1990s; and the reoccurrence of the Nembe crisis in 1996 and the renewed Eket crisis in 2000.

I will attempt to give an overview of oil exploration and exploitation in Etcheland, with a special focus on the callous Umuechem crisis of 1990.

The Umuechem Crisis of 1990

Umechem in Etche LGA has three sections, namely Umuoga, Umuogo and Umunwantu. The three Chiefs from each of these sections jointly rule Umuehem town which comprises of 12 compounds. SPDC discovered crude oil in Umuechem town in 1957. By April 1967, Umuechem had fourteen (14) oil wells, producing 31,865 barrels (Bonny Light)per day, representing 9.6 percent of the total production of old Rivers State. As at the time, the total production of old Rivers State was 332,201 barrels (i.e; 57.1 percent of the total national production per day). Inspite of this level of contribution to the national wealth, Umuechem community had no social amenities, or any infrastructure. The only tarred road in the area began at the end of the town enroute to the SPDCs oil wells (installations).

The people of Umuechem has made several representations and initiated dialogue with SPDC, including preparing a mutually beneficial Memorandum of Understanding (MoU), but to no avail. Compensation was hardly paid in cases of spillage which devastates water, farm land, and crops. In some cases SPDC could not finally avoid, the amount paid as compensation was too negligible to remedy the situation.

According to report, the entire Umuechem community met on 29 October 1990 and agreed to visit the SPDC oil locations to demand suspension of further development of the new wells it had struck. SPDC resisted the peaceful move and eventually invited the Nigeria Police Force (Mobil Unit) to the scene. On arrival, and characteristic of the Nigeria Police, they shot and killed Mr. Ojim (a youth). In retaliation, the mob also killed a policeman. In further retaliation the police came for mass arrest, and shot at sight anybody including women and children. Umuechem town was completely destroyed and deserted. Many people were killed, including Eze A.A Ordu Onye-Ishi-Agwuru, Igbo Clan and two of his children. The people found the decayed body of Chief A.A Ordu in his house after several days of unwanton destruction of the entire community.

It could be recalled that, the then Governor of old Rivers State, who is incidentally from Edo State ordered the Commander of Mobile Police (MOPOL) 07 to quickly quell the demonstration at "all cost". In the process of executing the "order", MOPOL 07 went to Umuechem and shot indiscriminately and killed about 520 persons of the community, mainly youths, women and senior citizens, including Eze A.A. Ordu himself. Thereafter, it became operation wipe them all.

The level of unwanton destruction which was unprecedented caused a national outcry and embarrassment to the State and Federal Military Governments. The then Military President, General Ibarahim .B. Babangada, directed that a Commission of inquiry be setup to investigate the matter. This was done. SPDC was persuaded and promised N10 million compensation, but due to bureaucracy, it could not be cleared on time, however, it made efforts to correct the anomaly. The effort, however, failed as SPDC was bent on deceiving the people. Unfortunately, the cheque has not been cleared to this day and the people were not compensated or assisted to rebuild their town.

The Umuechem case was the first in the history of oil and gas related conflicts which MNOC (SPDC), in partnership with Rivers State and the Federal Government so descended heavily on an unarmed oil producing community (OPC). It clearly showed that MNOCs are in partnership with Government in dealing with OPCs in the region, and the strategy of handling such crisis has since been confrontational, anchored on military action against the very citizens it (Government) pledged to defend in the first place. The study showed that this is still the predominant strategy in the industry. Thus, instead of preparing and negotiating an MoU, (SPDC and the other MNOCs) apply the policy of "divide-and-rule" and use the Paramount Rulers or Opinion Leaders to destabilize an entire community.

Athough the **Commission of Inquiry** submitted its Report and Rivers State Government issued a **White Paper,** the promised paltry compensation was not paid and the people bore alone the burden of rehabilitating and rebuilding their community. The Umuechem case was poorly handled and it became an eye-opener, signaling the beginning of conflicts between OPCs and MNOCs/Governments in the Region.

Although the Commission of Inquiry submitted its Report and Rivers State Government issued a White Paper, the promised paltry compensation was not paid and the people bore alone the burden of rehabilitating and rebuilding their community. The Umuechem case was poorly handled and it became an eye-opener, signaling the beginning of conflicts between OPCs and MNOCs/Governments in the Region.

Is Oil a Curse or a Blessing?
How can we explain a situation where what ought to be a blessing has now become a curse. A drive around all the Oil and Gas Producing Communities in Etchesland, such as Odagwa, Igbo, Umuebule, Ogkoroagu, Umuechem, Egwi, Umuakali and others clearly shows an environment overtaken by poverty and neglect. They live in squalor, while the territories occupied by the multinationals enjoy unlimited opulence. They have no accessible roads, no portable drinking water, no electricity and no healthcare facilities considering that air and environmental pollution

is automated. The children from these communities cannot afford quality and modern education. The standard of living is at its lowest ebb. I end this chapter with the following questions for whoever has an answer.

1. How will the minorities in Nigeria survive?
2. When will Etche be recognized and compensated?.
3. Who will lead this campaign of empowerment f o r Etche People?
4. When is the best time to begin this campaign?

As I pose these fundamental question, it is indeed choosing one case against many to show how minority people suffer in the hands of Nigerian government ran by majority groups.

CHAPTER FOUR

THE ROAD TO THE FUTURE

All great movements are popular movement. They are the volcanic eruption of human passion and emotions, stirred into activity by the ruthless goddess of distress or by the touch of spoken word cast into the midst of the people.

-Adolf Hitler

The Fourth Republic was ushered in by Gen Abdulsalami Abubakar in 1999. He handed over the reins of power to Chief Olusegun Obasanjo of the Peoples Democratic Party (PDP). In Rivers State, Group Captain Sam Ewang, who was the Military Administrator, handed over to Dr. Peter Odili, also of the PDP.

Since the inception of the Fourth Republic, the PDP-led government, both at the state and federal levels has done less in the projection of Etche political identity. Outside Etche statutory positions, the highest position which any Etche son/daughter has merited in the 16 years of this republic is the position of Commissioners and Head of Service, occupied by Dame Esther Anucha. Thus, we have become politically stagnant.

In a paper published by the foremost Socio-political organization in Etcheland, *Etche Heritage*

Foundation entitled:- **Rivers State Governorship Race 2015: Where is Etche in The Slate?,** the group wrote:

"*Is a topsy-turvy affair again in the now all too familiar political rumble.   The time for the emergence of the polity: the political analysts and pundits; political juggernauts; political aspirants and king makers; political posturing and negotiations; the jingles; and even some sabre-rattling.*

Against this backdrop and most importantly, is the emergence of the senatorial and ethnic drumbeats. At stake as usual are the seats of the governor, deputy governor, senators and some federal representations that span multiple local government areas.

Also simultaneously, saliently at stake are the very high non-elective government post-election offices of the SSG, Chief of Staff, Speaker of the H o u s e   o f   A s s e m b l y ,   s o m e   k e y commissionerships, and other appointments at the state and federal levels.

In political parlance, this set of political offices is called a slate; a slate headed by the governor and the political rumble is about filling this slate. Persons to occupy this slate are generally constituted in such a way that they are or zoned distributed or zoned equitably over senatorial and ethnic .divides to reflect a fair representation across the board. It is a peculiar and an important situation that in Rivers State, senatorial and ethnic dimensions are not orthogonal or distinct; they are intertwined.

Rivers State is the home to many of the ethnic minorities of the Niger Delta Ijaw, Ikwerre, Ekpeye, Ogba, Etche, Ogoni, Igbo and so on. In Rivers State, the riverine-upland dichotomy is also used to distinguish the terrain of the Ijaws (who occupy Andoni, Bonny, Kalabari, Okrika/Ogu-Bolo, Opobo, Abua/Odual, parts of Ahoada West, Port Harcourt and Oyigbo) from the terrain of other ethnic groups. While senatorial groupings of past republics have been arbitrary with no consideration for ethnic homogeneity, it is significant to note that in the current three senatorial districts of East, South-East and West, each was ensured to be a combination of riverine (Ijaw) and upland ethnic groups.

Thus, senatorial East has upland Etche and Ikwerre together with Ijaw Okrika and Ogu-Bolo; South-East has upland Ogoni with Ijaw Andoni, Opobo and parts of Oyigbo; and West has Ogba, Egbema, Ndoni and Ekpeye along with Ijaw Bonny, Kalabari, Abua/Odual and parts of Ahoada West.

It is important to note that in the arbitrariness of these senatorial groupings, not only are ethnic groups and their domiciliation in a senatorial zone not homogenous, they also do not have to be geographically adjacent or contiguous.

Thus, for instance, in East, Etche has no common boundary with Okrika and in senatorial West, Ogba-land has no common boundary with Degema. In this arbitrary grouping also is the general undertone of whether a senatorial district is heavily riverine or skewed upland.

Thus, in this mix, the question of whether the zoning of the governorship slot should be based on senatorial or upland-riverine dichotomy is not as simple as it may sound.

Other dimensions also come to play in the filling of the slate: the issue of the population of the various ethnic groups, the locations of the heavy population centres and the differential contribution to the economy of the state also become major factors. Herein lays the story of throes and of woes of Etche ethnic nationality in this complex situation beginning with the introduction of the presidential system in the second republic: Etche has virtually and completely been omitted from the slates!

Etche, as a distinct ethnic nationality (domiciled in Etche and Omuma local government areas), is upland and currently in the East senatorial district.

As it turns out, no matter how the senatorial and ethnic factors have been diced, sliced, mixed, blended and mashed, Etche has not been part of the slate and there have been a total of eight elections (and nine slates) two in the second republic, two in the third republic and four in the current fourth republic. In the second republic of Shagari, Etche was in the Ahoada senatorial district spanning Ahoada East & West, Abua/Odual, Ogba, Egbema, Ndoni, Ikwerre, Emohua, Etche and Omuma. In the first election of 1979, the governor was Melford Okilo and Etche was represented by late Distinguished Senator, Chief Francis Ellah of Ogba-land and the second election of 1983 saw Okilo return but now with Senator Victor Odili of Ndoni representing Etche senatorially.

Even in the confused, thorny, missteps and truncated elections of the third republic starting in 1992, Etche was never in the slate. Rufus Ada-

George of Okrika became Governor. Senatorially, Etche found herself grouped with Khana, Gokana, Ikwerre, Emohua, Obio/Akpor, Oyigbo, Tai-Eleme.

It was the Distinguished Senator, Dr. Bennet Birabi of Ogoni, that represented this district in 1992. In the second election of 1997, the senatorial groupings were different and Etche found herself with Ikwerre and Okrika in what was then and now the East senatorial district and was represented by Noble Chukumati of Ikwerre.

This current fourth republic has had four elections but five slates with the governors: Peter Odili of Ndoni (twice), Celestine Omehia of Ikwerre (five months),and Rotimi Amaechi (twice). The senatorial district (East) in which Etche is, remains the same as in the second half of the third republic with John Mbata of Ikwerre (twice) and George Sekibo of Okrika (twice) representing this zone. Thus, overall, Etche has been senatorially represented by Ogba, Ogoni, Ndoni, Ikwerre and Ijaw Okrika i.e., senators from everywhere else but Etche.

Thus, for Etche, the arbitrariness of the various senatorial groupings has resulted in very unfavourable and dire outcomes associated with absence from active participation in the politics of the state, least of which is marginalization.

Etche has also been noticeably absent in post-election slots in the slates. Etche has had no SSG, Chief of Staff, Speaker of the House of Assembly and other significant appointments at the state and federal levels. Etche is so excluded that even when the position of national deputy speaker was twice zoned to Rivers State in the House of Representatives, Etche was skipped and instead, these slots went to Ekpeye and Ikwerre. Slots of federal minister, ambassador, presidential advisors and headship of federal parastatals have all eluded Etche also.

Herein rests the justification for Etche to vie for all positions in the slate and most importantly the position of governor, to correct the political neglect that Etche has endured for over a span of forty years. The position of senate is long overdue for Etche and has been argued in various quarters before now and justifiably so.

A quick enumeration here will suffice to highlight the gross absence of Etche from the slates: Ijaws have produced two (civilian) presidential advisers, heads of parastatals, SSGs, speakers of the House of Assembly, ambassadors, etc.; Ogonis have produced many senators, SSGs, ministers, presidential adviser, etc.; the Ndonis and Ogbas have produced governor, senators and ministers; Ikwerres have produced governors, senators, speaker, ambassador, deputy speaker at the house of representatives; we can go on. Etche is nil and arguably at the bottom rung of the linear ethnic nationality scale!

As of today again, in a potential repeat performance, there is a looming irony in what is glaringly ominously hellish for Etche: in the current political rumble, not only is there clamour by many of these other accomplished ethnic nationalities Ijaws, Ogonis, Ikwerres for the governorship position, Etche appears not to be in the fray.

This same Etche who by virtue of decades of neglect, Etche by virtue of her contribution to the economy of the state (arguably the second largest producer of oil and gas with 250 producing oil wells), Etche by virtue of her large population, (1.2 million) and landmass (1300 square km, the second largest in the state) and Etche, by virtue of her comparably teeming large manpower base (doctors, engineers, lawyers, accountants, managers, politicians, etc. with a significant number in the Diaspora) must and should imperatively be at the forefront of this current political rumble.

The time is here for a correction; whether it is by selection or election, it is time Etche is factored in: If the governorship is zoned to the upland or to East senatorial, then it has to be Etche. Hence, this is a call to Etche to participate in the current political rumble and it is also a reminder to the rest of the state, the kingmakers in particular, to the plight and neglect suffered by Etche and the need for a correction to make Etche feel part of this great state. Let the pundits, juggernauts and jingles chant to this and Etche aspirants should emerge. Etche has to be in the slate this time and that is why they should not hem 'n' haw but scream, as others, for not to, will guarantee a continued existence in servitude."

As a people, we have a peculiar problem in Rivers State. We are constantly underrated and demeaned; our gentle and non-violent disposition is seen as inferiority complex and our efforts lack courage and sacrifice. If, as a people, we wish to make an impact in the affairs of this multi-ethnic state and agglomerate nation, then we must review our political philosophy and public relations. We have to be more courageous and less fearful. We must bear in mind that it is not the Etche, which we are, that causes us to be underrated and demeaned, but rather, the Etche that others perceive us to be due to our actions or inactions.

Therefore, our route to political acceptance and social esteem does not lie in the denial of the fact, but more in the emasculation of other people's perception of us by taking decisive and coordinated steps aimed at grabbing power.

The Etche and Niger Delta people must advance into the mainstream of Nigerian politics. Isolationism and wallowing in an orgy of self-pity or indeed carrying the banner of protest is counter-productive. If we persist in complaining, weeping, wailing and bemoaning of our fate, we risk the bitter-sweet taste of drowning in the brackish waters of our tears. The Etche and Niger Delta people must face the future with the full courage which our Nigerian citizenship bestows upon us. We must move forward with optimism and ignore the doomsday rantings of some of our brothers.

As we approach the next political elections, let me say very clearly that no ethnocentric concept of political organization has a chance in today's Nigeria. Such a concept is no longer viable. It is sterile and retrograde. I am aware that already, this area is littered with so many organizations, all surreptitiously trying to steal a march ahead of others, trying to beat the gun as it were. Whilst wishing luck to every political group, let me hasten to remind everyone that the people of this area will not be high-jacked by forces either from within or without.

The purpose of the ongoing political exercise is to discover and establish a system of government that will enhance the quality of life for the common people at the grassroots. The name of the game is grassroot: rural populace, farmers, wine tappers, traders, pupils, teachers, washermen and women, fishermen and women, taxi and lorry drivers, bus drivers, nurses, and midwives, labourers, the unemployed, widows and orphans, police, soldiers, etc. The foregoing should be the focus of our political attention, not who shall be what.

CHAPTER FIVE

LEADERSHIP QUESTION

It is by what we ourselves have done, and not by what others have done for us, that we shall be remembered in after ages.

-Francis Wayland.

In every age, there comes a time when leadership must come forth to meet the needs of the hour. Therefore, there is no potential leader who does not find his time. Tragically, there are times when no leader arises. Since a nation is only as great as her leaders, we need to exercise great care in choosing our leaders.

Our democratic rights must be used in such a way as to ensure that the right persons are chosen to lead. We must not confuse champions for leaders, nor prominence for pre-eminence. We must not confuse eloquence for honesty; neither must we confuse silence for wisdom. We must not confuse good looks for efficiency nor bravado for courage.

What kind of leaders do we need? The leadership that Niger Delta people need must meet the following criteria. We need leaders who are servants of the people, not their masters. We need leaders who will serve first the common man. We require leaders who will ensure fairness and equity to the various villages and communities in Niger Delta region.

We need leaders who must be the embodiment of honour and at all times, exemplify the ideals of our people. We need leaders who will keep alive the flames of our communal aspirations. We want leaders who will be trusted friends of the people and protectors of the disadvantaged and oppressed. We require leaders who will have the right judgment both of people and of situations.

We need leaders who will attract the right kind of lieutenants and who must be accountable to Niger Delta people and are subjected to the collective will of the people. We need leaders who must be fanatical for Niger Delta people's welfare and must, at all times, stand for justice and symbolize good governance.

We want leaders who will posses the ability to inspire the people out of despondency. We need leaders who can submerge excessive personal prestige and who are not vain glorious. What Niger Delta people need is a proper sense of direction.

It is of interest to make a brief assessment of how the various ethnic groups in Rivers State have faired in matters of leadership since the advent of the Fourth

Republic in 1999. Among the Riverine Ijaw Group, a new forceful leadership quickly emerged, more or less on consensus. They have produced Senators, Deputy Governors, Ambassadors, Ministers, Speakers of RSHA, Party leaders both at the state and national level.

Among the Ikwerres, a formula was not difficult to find either, for everyone who has eyes could see who their leaders are. In 1999, Rt. Hon. Chibuike Rotimi Amaechi emerged the speaker and by 2007, he became the Governor of Rivers State. In 1999, Late Amb. Ignatious Ajuru was appointed ambassador to Gabon and re-appointed to Ukraine in 2003. In 2003, Rt. Hon. Austin Opara emerged Deputy Speaker of the House of Representatives. In 1999 and 2003, Sen. John Mbata was elected the Senator representing Rivers East Senatorial District. In 2011, Barr. Nyesom Ezenwo Wike was appointed a Minister of the Federal Republic of Nigeria. Presently, Barr. Wike has also emerged the Governor of Rivers State, although surrounded with both zoning and electoral controversy.

The Ogonis have gone global with the struggle for , economic, social and political justice and equity. They have produced three Senators - Sens. Lee Maeba , Magnus Abe and Olaka Nwogu. They have been appointed Secretary to Government of Rivers State four times since 1999 - Hons. Magnus Abe, Gabriel Pidomson, George Feyii and Keneth Kobani.

The Orashis have produced a governor in the person of Dr. Peter Odili and have consistently led the PDP for several years - Chief G.U Ake and Bro Felix Obuah. They have produced two Senators - Sen Wilson Ake and Osinachukwu Ideozu. They have also produced Deputy Speaker of House of Representative - Rt. Hon. Chibudom Nwuche.

The Etches, unfortunately, have not fared so well. Beyond our statutory positions such as House of Representative, Assembly, Local Government Chairmanship, and commissioners, we have nothing serious to our credit.

Perhaps, it is one of those ironies in modern Rivers political development, that when at last the Fourth Republic was ushered in, Etche people, caught unawares, were unable to find a true Etche leadership. Those who could have offered genuine leadership were either too apprehensive or too lethargic to come forward. As a result, the Etche people found themselves, by sheer default, carrying the heavy burden of a bunch of opportunists who could not, by any stretch of the imagination, be described as Etche leaders. Yes! Yes!! Yes!!!

The picture we see cannot do us proud. Where is the pride in having leaders who cannot create opportunities for the development of Etche and its people? There is no pride whatever, in having leaders who have constantly turned their backs on Etche people in their hour of need and distress. We do not want leaders who do not value us; leaders who would rather use us than subject themselves permanently to the collective will of our people.

We should no longer tolerate leaders who think that leadership is merely a game of chance. We have no need for leaders who spend more time in clubs and midnight parties than in attending to the affairs of our people, neither those who have proved that they can be juvenile in every inch of their conduct, suited to be band managers.

Leadership, I believe, is a business for serious minds. We do not want leaders who are erratic, inimical and vindictive because they lack the maturity required for leadership. Leaders should not be ignorant of the basic tenets of democracy to the extreme point of referring to our people as weaklings. In a democracy, such as ours, the people are the masters and the leaders their servants.

Those who hold positions of trust must be alive to the true demands of responsibility. The incursion of party politics into the Etche cultural heritage brought about a destructive by-products. It corrupted the system of pan-Etche identity by seizing the machinery of the cultural unions, abolishing consensus as a basic Etche pattern of civil administration and instituting personality cults.

The Etche system of consensus had religious roots, and there were sanctions against *'he aru'* (an abomination) as Etche people know it. By establishing his authority over this cultural   religious heritage, the politician elected himself a mini Holy Roman Empire, with powers over the temporal and spiritual lives of Etche people.

Our political system in Etche land should be revitalized by the resuscitation of the Etche cultural union - Ogbako Etche and that union should play its role as a check on the excesses of politicians who may wish to substitute their personal ambitions for the interests of all Etche people in a unified and prosperous Nigeria.

All Etche people should join hands in defiance of their past failures. Etche people should resist the attempt of their own brothers and sisters to write them off in the history of this country by proclaiming from roof tops that all that Etche people need is an identity. Any Etche person, who sincerely believes that his ethnic group lives on identity alone, in the modern day and age, is clearly naïve.

ABSOLUTE POWER CORRUPTS LEADERS

On the question of leadership, let me, at risk of sounding trite, say again, that "power corrupts and absolute power corrupts absolutely."

Every effort should be made to discourage and prevent the emergence of a personality cult at all levels of authority. Personality cult, in a fissiparous, pluralistic, competitive society such as ours, can only exacerbate jealously and breed unproductivity. Time has come for power in Etche rather than the prerogative of an individual member of a competing and sometimes mutual antagonistic group.

The new Etche leader must be the embodiment of the Etche people's aspirations. Part of his role as leader should be to maintain the morale of the people at all times. To be a friend of the people, their protector and the guardian of their dreams. He should have the right judgment both of people and of situations and the ability to attract to himself the right kind of lieutenants who can better the people's interest.

The new leader must not only say but always demonstrate that the power he exercises is derived from the people. Like every Nigerian public servant, he must be constantly accountable, whether in office or out of office. He must be accountable to the people for the use he made of their mandate. He must get out when the people ask him to get out. The more power the new leader is given by the people, the less his personal freedom and the greater his responsibility for the good of the people. He should always take decisions in favour of the poor and disadvantaged in our midst

He must be sensitive to the pain and aguish of the people. He must laugh with them in their joy and cry with them in their sorrow. He should never allow his high office to separate him from the people's welfare. The new Etche leader must be an adept in the protection of the weak, the disadvantaged and poor.

The new Etche leader must, at all times, stand for justice in dealing with the people. He must lean backwards, if need be, to protect the innocent. He must constantly insist that it is better for a guilty person to go free rather than to have an innocent person suffer. He should be the symbol of justice, which is the supreme guarantee of good governance.

He should be ready, if need be, to lay down his life in courage and must be able to inspire people out of despondency. The new Etche leader must be an extremist in the defence of Etche interest.

The new Etche leader should never strive towards the perpetuation of his office or devise means to cling to office beyond the clear mandate of the people. A leader who serves his people well will be enshrined in the hearts and minds of his people. He must strive, at all times, to be the symbol of excellence. He is the quintessential Etcheman.

LAST WORD ON LEADERSHIP
(1)   One essential demand of leadership is to be like a waste paper basket, a dustbin where all dirt and   rubbish are heaped. Whoever is not ready to accept s   u   c   h treatment does not qualify to be our leader. A   l e a d e r must be prepared to have rubbish heaped on   h i s head.

(2)   As Etche moves steadfastly on the road to becoming a developed and united people, there comes a dire

need for leaders who will perceive the entire Etche territory and her people as their own people. Every leader must have a dream and be steadfast in his efforts to fulfill that dream.

(3)   Service to a people is not a profession. It is a vocation and a leader must make a lot of sacrifices for it.

A leader does not complain when things are not going too well since that is one of the occupational hazards. A leader must not try to cushion himself (by amassing wealth) against the future. Though the temptation is great, there is nothing more counterproductive in leadership than corruption.

A leader, apart from constantly reassuring his people, must always make himself acceptable to every one. To do this, he has to be above board in all his dealings.

CHAPTER SIX

THE NEW DIRECTION

*A politician thinks of
the next election;
a statesman thinks of
the next generation*

- James Freeman Clarke

The new direction I now propose is a road where the Etcheman will cease to be his own worst enemy; a road that leads right into the center of the questionable Nigeria; a road that will ensure the national cake, once jointly baked by all Nigerians, will be shared equally by all Nigerians, which includes the Etches.

I would like to see the patriots of our land devoted to untrumpeted service, knowing that recognition will come in due time. It is true that they also serve those who sit and watch, but there is so much to do that the Etche people cannot spare even one idle spectator.

In this regard, I would commend you to John Gardner's remarks in his book, **No Easy Victories.** He said;

> *"Our prospects never looked brighter, and the problems never looked tougher. Anyone who is not stirred by both of these statements is too tired to be of much use to us in the days ahead."*

During elections, you and I will always be called upon, once again, to make a choice. Our duty is clear. We have to ensure that we elect at all levels men and women capable of protecting our true interests. We have to return, both at the executive and legislative levels, a party that can best assist us to secure our best interests.

Politics, as we all know, is a science of leverage, and leverage is an art of numbers. For this reason, I urge you to ensure that whoever represents us, and at whatever level, has the requisite numbers to exert the requisite leverage. At the executive level, this means a large legislative majority. At the legislative level, it means enormous grass-root support.

As a people, our basic interest at this time can be listed under three main headings:

(a) To ensure that our structural presence in Rivers State and Nigeria is revatalized.

If we are to attract the attention of the state and nation and develop our resources, receive more appointments and allocation, then it goes without saying that we must control a number of local government, wards and unit commensurate with our relative numerical strength in Rivers State as an ethnic group.

(b) To ensure Etche people get equal opportunities in structural terms.

As a people, we do not accept to be confined to the status of second class citizenship in our beloved state. Proudly, we dispute any claim of a greater love for Rivers State or Nigeria by any group within the state or country. We therefore cannot support any organization, political or otherwise, which does not envisage the possibility of an Etche man, one day, becoming the Governor of Rivers State, Minister, Senator, Ambassador or the President of the Federal Republic of Nigeria. A party or politician that envisages that, but has no chance of winning an election, is clearly a non-starter.

(c) We are proud people, perhaps the proudest, in this land. So we must seek to collaborate with the group or the political party in Rivers State that gives us full acceptance rather than tolerance.

Whatever party we vote for must accept that we have an absolute right to choose our own leaders. These were our political requirements in 1999 and in the years to come. On these should be based our choice at all elections.

Rivers State and Nigeria are multi-national states. Etche people are one nation within this family of nations. With such a political demography, a cardinal principle in Etche geo-politics must be the assertion of our right and protection of our interest while according similar rights to all the other nationalities that comprise Rivers State and Nigeria at large.

We have not seen it so clearly in the past, because we put party affiliation before a scientific view of Etche geo-politics. Indeed, the sequence should have been in reverse - a sound knowledge of Etche geo-politics determining our party affiliation.

We therefore need an ideological revolution, a new overview of Rivers State politics. And to sustain this new perspective, our people, collectively and as individuals, need a new behavourial pattern that is appropriate to it. Once we define and grasp this ideological revolution, we can then rationally chart our path in Rivers State politics. Political forums founded on a 'siege' mentality that erupts in confrontation with everything non-Etche is no road. It will lead to isolation, 'political arthritis', and hence defeat.

Ethnic alliances, however subtly camouflaged under the cloak of political arrangement are not a way out either. Such alliances are inherently unstable. They provoke counter alliances with the result that Rivers State is perennially in danger of falling apart along ethnic seams. Above all, the expediencies resorted to in sustaining the administration of such alliances, as well as the intrigues hatched in an effort to destabilize such administrations, mean that the welfare of the people is invariably relegated to the background.

The correct way forward for us is a free and principled interaction with all Rivers people, regulated by respect for fundamental human rights, the rule of law, courage and the guarantee of equality of opportunities for all.

It is therefore the specific role of government, at all times, to sustain and nurture the Nigerian constitution and constantly expand areas of our national life where the principle of equality of opportunities for all Nigerians can fully operate. We have to secure these conditions in Etche and Omuma Local Government Areas. But, even more importantly, we have to join hands with people to secure these conditions all over Rivers State, for such a new Rivers State is a condition for the true well being of all Etche people.

We owe it as a duty to ourselves, not only to participate in Nigerian public life, but also to participate in such a manner as to demonstrate, in concrete terms and not in mere verbal protestations, that we have parted for ever with disunity and selfishness.

If we fail to perform in this way, we will continue to surround ourselves and all our actions with the clouds of ineptitude and division.

For Etche to grow, we must chart a new direction. Mature, constructive and purposeful approach to issues affecting the interest of our people, I believe, this is what politics should be about. As a people, we cannot fulfill our communal aspirations, aims and hopes until we move away from divide- and-rule tactics at the state level and personality politics at the local level, to politics of issues.

The task ahead is great and requires the involvement of all of us in the service of our beloved Etche land.

SECTION TWO

PROGRESS AND REGRESS

In the confrontation between the stream and the rock, the stream always wins, not through strength but by perseverance.

-H. Jackson Brown

CHAPTER SEVEN

WHEN THE
BLOOD CRIES

---◆-------◆---

All labour that uplifts humanity has dignity and importance and should be undertaken with painstaking excellence.

-Dr. Martin Luther King, Jr

---◆-------◆---

As I write this book, many communities in Niger Delta region are under serious violent communal cum political crisis. From communities in Delta to Bayelsa to Akwa Ibom to Rivers and others. In Rivers State, some Ikwerre communities, Etche area, Kalabari zone, Ogoni axis and Orashi region are all flash points.

For the purpose of this work, we shall restrict our discussion to the Etche situation. There is what I may describe as "internal-war" in Etcheland. Okehi, Igbodo, Akwa, Ulakwo, Obibi, Akwu-Obor, Umuaturu, Mba, Ndashi are very volatile. The people of these villages live at the mercy of their sons who ought to be their hope for a better tomorrow. People are killed, molested and harassed on a daily basis without thorough resistance from the authorities, maybe because of political interference in security matters.

Let me share a story of an incidence that took place

sometimes ago. During the 2009 December Christmas season, a football match was organized in Isu town. During the football tournament, a minor quarrel ensued between some groups of boys from Ozuzu and Isu. The conflict resulted in fighting and use of matchet by the parties involved. The injured persons were rushed to the hospital for treatment. But that is not the end of story.

As soon as the initial fight was over and those who were part of the separation and settlement of the quarrel dispersed to their various homes, the worst happened. The other group of boys from Ozuzu town who felt defeated because one of them sustained serious injury through matchet cut, mobilized for another round of attack. According to the report, they laid ambush at Ozuzu to retaliate the attack on anybody from Isu, not minding if he was part of initial quarrel or not.

In a few minutes, a young boy of about 24 years from Isu was on his way home that evening, when the squad suddenly pounced on him. The squad was armed with machetes and other dangerous weapons, so they used the machetes on the young man until his stomach was cut open. The intestines poured out like an animal that is being butchered in the slaughter for consumption. As soon as the assailants saw that he was dead, they flew out of sight, thinking that they would never be discovered. Unknown to them, the young man did not die immediately.

Good Samaritans carried him to a nearby hospital for first aid. In the process of administering first aid, he mentioned the names of the assailants. Sad to inform you, that the young boy did not survive the first aid. He passed on as soon as he was able to disclose the identity of those who attacked him as if he was a wild animal, being chased by desperate hunters.

As soon as the news of his death got to the ears of his kith and kin at Isu town, they immediately mobilized for another revenge mission. Armed with different weapons of war, they stormed Ozuzu town in search of the murders.

They made straight to their compounds. As was expected, the murderers had disappeared into the thin air. Left with no other choice, they decided to attack their houses. In less than an hour, over ten houses were burnt down, including the properties in the houses. None of the murderers owned any of those houses. The houses and properties that were burnt down belonged to their parents.

To enable on-the-spot assessment of the damage done as a result of the minor quarrel between the young men, a visit to Ozuzu was made. In one of the compounds that was visited, I was shocked by the sight of an old man of about eighty years old. He owned one of the houses that were destroyed. His son was among those fingered in the murder of the young man. As at the time of my visit, the old man had no place to stay in his own community. The house that took him years to build had been destroyed in a twinkle of an eye because of the stupidity of his child. What a sad story.

In 2009, Umuechem community witnessed another round of communal crisis sparked off by chieftaincy tussle. The crisis witnessed loss of lives; houses and properties worth millions of naira were destroyed. As a measure to curtail the crisis, the entire indigenes of Umuechem were asked to vacate their ancestral home. They were forcefully driven out of their land by security operatives who were mandated to restore peace to the area. As at the time of writing this book, it is pertinent to mention that the people have since been restored to their community, but the negative and ugly effect of the crisis may linger for some time.

Few years ago, precisely in 2001, Umuonyia Community in Egwi autonomous community had its own fair, or do I say sad share of communal crisis. Houses were destroyed and some people were forced out to become refugees. The matter has since been resolved by the court of law and the council of chiefs, but it is sad to mention that the scar left by the crisis has not completely healed.

These examples are just few among the numerous cases of communities torn apart in Etche land as a result of avoidable crises. There are other reported cases of serious communal crises that are yet to be resolved. For example, Odagwa community had their own sad share of communal crisis in 2009. Several houses were destroyed and lives lost. As at the time of writing this book, the crisis has not been fully resolved.

The questions that we all need to answer are: What exactly are we fighting for? Development or destruction? Who are we supposed to be fighting? Ourselves or the Nigerian state and oil companies that have deprived us of development? Can we achieve the Next Etche Development Project (NEDEP) through the instruments of violence and war? I leave every Etche son and daughter to think and give me the answers to these questions, bearing this Yoruba proverb in mind: "The sword does not recognize the head of the blacksmith who made it."

IDENTIFIED CAUSES OF CRISIS IN

From investigation on the causes of the crises experienced in Etche in the past ten years, it is discovered that the identified causes are: chieftaincy tussle, land dispute, political tussle, proceeds from oil companies and clash of interests.

On Chieftaincy Tussle

Contest for chieftaincy position has been identified as one of the major causes of crisis in Etche land. Agreed that such chieftaincy crisis is not synonymous with Etche people, but there are other ethnic nationalities that have never had such crisis in the past. Position and titles, it is believed, are temporal. They are more temporal than the flowers in the field. The moment a man is dead, his position and title is also dead with him, what lives on are his good deeds and the legacy he left behind.

The desperate pursuit of position will always lead to crisis. Sincerity of purpose and maturity are required if peaceful chieftaincy installation is to be achieved in Etcheland. People should learn to be truthful in chieftaincy related issues rather than supporting the best bidder.

On Land Disputes

Land is a precious commodity. It is the pillar upon which other factors of development are sustained. Land, never depreciates, it appreciates. All over the world, land is treasure.

However, despite the value that land commands, especially in Etcheland, as it is part of our traditional heritage, it should not generate crisis. The privileged often use financial means to obtain witness to disposes the less privileged of their land. People should find a means of resolving land disputes to avoid crises that may degenerate to destruction of lives. It is pathetic that most elders in the villages can be bought with a "piece of cake" to become false witnesses.

On Proceeds from Companies

It is the responsibility of tenant companies to fulfill their be proper documented agreement between the companies and their host communities. This agreement must be honored by the tenant companies to avoid unwarranted attack from the host communities.

On the other hand, the various host communities must agree on how best to invest the proceeds from the tenant companies. The communities should invest the proceeds in a project that will benefit the general public, rather than sharing the money among the various individuals within the community. The Community Development Committee members must be people of unquestionable character.

Moreover some concerned citizens of Etche should meet and prepare a model MOU for all host communities, because some communities doesn't have the requisite knowledge to prepare adequate MOU.

On Political Differences

We cannot all be in the same political association. Politics is a game of choice. Ideally, it is game of like minds. You follow the association where your ideology and intrest is being represented. Democracy recognizes and demands that people should be allowed to identify with the political association of their choice. On politics, Etche people should endeavor to reinforce Ogbako Etche to make it responsive and effective in political matters. Some of our politicians have become monsters and need to be tamed by some kind of political education and criticisms.

Churches can even assist in political education and awareness.

But, it is rather unfortunate that instead of political diversity to promote healthy political participation and practice, violence has continued to be at the center of political crisis. What is supposed to bring unity has been converted to an instrument of disunity.

On our differences

There are no two people who are the same. Even identical twin are not the same. Their choices, desires, ambitions are completely different from each other. Their thoughts and impressions of life are peculiar and unique. We are diverse and different as individuals.

Therefore, let us find the universality in our diversity. Our individual differences ought to be the medium of our unity and not disunity.

Let me say that the effort to achieve a reorientation of Etche attitudes in this dispensation is not being hinged on any political party. My appeal in this regard is directed at Etche people of all political persuasion. I respect the right of anyone to belong to the political party of his/her choice.

It is a development that cuts across party lines. We are sadly witnessing an upsurge of the politics of patronage in place of the politics of patriotism. It is a phenomenon that has pitched brother against brother, kith against kin, in a do-or-die battle to secure a ring-side seat around the power stage. Those who lend themselves to these weaknesses are many. They often fall victims to the deceit of elements whose decisions are meant to weaken the Etches as a group. Some weaknesses are clearly unpardonable, because they negatively affect the collective guard of the Etche people and create opportunities for the group to be exploited.

The patriots of our land should be sent to rendering devoted and selfless service, knowing that recognition will come in due time. For those who sit and watch, there is so much to do that Etche people cannot spare even one idle spectator.

CHAPTER EIGHT

WALKING THE PATH OF PEACE AND UNITY

I refuse to accept the view that mankind is so tragically bound to the starless midnight of racism and war that the bright day break of peace and brotherhood can never become a reality.... I believe that unarmed truth and unconditional love will have the final word.

Dr. Martin Luther King, Jr.

Peace is the panacea for development in any society. Without peace, there will never be accelerated development. Peace is the foundation upon which development is built, and sustained. No society has even achieved recognizable progress without peace. We all need peace in Etche if we are to make head way. It is a common knowledge that violence will do no good to any man.

I have been privileged to travel to various parts of this country, and have made the following observations;

(1)   Development is never achieved through violence.
(2)   Everybody is a loser after each round of crisis.
(3)   Peace and dialogue are the panacea for development.

From the above observation, it is obvious that the projection of The Next Etche Development Project

(NEDEP) demands our collective resolve to give peace a chance. We must make the decision as a people to continually pursue every opportunity for peace.

For peace to reign in Etche, our people must discover a requisite cure for her cancer. Like all search for medical cure, the effort has to follow the standard methods of prevention, control and cure. The business of finding an urgent cure to Etche's illness is the business of all Etche people. We need expertise in this direction even though there had been no experts hitherto.

We all have to agree that nobody, no group, no government appointee, intellectual, political movement, man or woman, student, or any of the various interest groups in the land has a monopoly of wisdom. Whenever we predestinate a group as the repository of wisdom, the only fact is that wisdom resides outside that selected group. Etche people cannot afford a policy of exclusion; it is most counter-productive.

The crisis affecting Etche people is too deep rooted, and consequences so alarming, that we cannot, and must not waste too much time in an orgy of self-flagelation.

Our inability to solve the problem of unity is a major obstacle to the progress of our society. It is this lack of unity that has turned Etche land into a battle field and which has unleashed all the primitive instincts that result in war. In Etche, we have failed to evolve a society. Rather, at every stage of our social intercourse, there have been the victor, the vanquished and the resistant.

Another factor which retards the desired progress in the emergence of a new Etche society is that our socio-cultural organizations and traditional institutions are very fragile. This fact is further compounded by the fact that most of the actors on the political scene have but scanty experience in the system they have to operate.

We have witnessed the continued deterioration of our society. We know that empty platitudes cannot solve our problems, and neither can grotesque posturing. Regrettably, we have to realize that if in Etche, reform from the top becomes impossible, then we must gird our loins to face a revolution from the bottom. I do not believe there is an exclusive way; neither can I accept that one person possesses all the answers. For this one reason, I cannot support persons.

Rather, I have continued to search for a perfect idea to support and the best pattern to follow peace. All indications point, at this moment in our development, towards peaceful society and ideal democratic practice.

Etche people cannot make progress without peace and unity. Etche cannot fulfill her mission to all her people without peace and unity. Etche cannot lead, nor can she .

have a decisive voice in the comity of nations without unity. We need unity and peace. A discussion in Etche, as a people, cannot be considered complete without mention of Ogbako Etche. It is pertinent at this point to mention that Ogbako Etche, which is the apex socio-cultural organization of Etche people, must live up to its responsibility. Ogbako Etche must demonstrate by words and action that it has the ability to facilitate and reintroduce peace in all communities in Etche. This, I believe, must be done in partnership with the council of traditional rulers and political office holders.

Etche people will breakthrough and prosper only through internal peace, stability and cohesion. This is the beginning of wisdom. Etche can only be great if she can maintain peace within her borders.

I have purposely left many questions unanswered and have not made propositions. In a way, what I have offered is a dialogue, a list of issues which should become subject for a longer discussion. Sometimes, I have given one side-of the coin and at other times, I have given the reverse: the thesis and then the anti-thesis. Rarely have I presumed upon a synthesis.

My aim is to provoke a dialogue. I would wish, in this dialogue, to act simply as a gadfly. This dialogue is vital to our progress as a people and must remain a constant exercise.

CHAPTER NINE

OUR POLITICAL LANDMINES

Who passively accepts evil is as much involved in it as he who helps it. He who accepts evil without protesting against it is really cooperating with it

- Martin L. king Jr.

The problem with Etche land is that she is embroiled in political crisis. The root causes of the crisis, are greed and selfishness. Most Etche sons and daughters who are privileged to be in leadership positions have allowed personal interest to overtake collective interest.

The politics of hand-picking, as against the democratic process, has obviously resulted in political crisis. We have watched, aghast how our youths have taken up arms against one another in the name of politics. Our present political practice is akin to a house on fire, it is surely in dire need of a fire brigade.

Each government and politician in Etche ascended the seat of power on the premise that it would produce the elusive unity. Each government, in turn, crashed because it failed to produce the much sought-after unity. Rather than produce unity, they have become the architects of crisis and disunity! What then is this unity and why does it elude us?.

I have read about battles; and have heard of carnage. I have reflected on all these and have come to the conclusion that all is vain; that warfare solves nothing. We cannot dominate; all we can do is to accommodate. While I was writing this chapter, I had the opportunity of going through the Holy Bible and, as I thought of Etche, one passage came to my memory, a verse that says: *"if a house be divided against itself, that house cannot stand"*. In a nutshell, this is the problem of Etche. If Etche be divided against itself, Etche cannot stand.

You will appreciate my reluctance in expressing my opinion at this moment in view of the present political confusion in Etche. Yet because we are Etche people; because of the deep concern I feel for Etche, and because I cannot hide my fears for Etche, I will put a few propositions with the hope that these will provoke wider debate and more analysis of predicament.

What then is political unity? Unity in a political unit, is a state where the entire polity is completely reconciled with itself: a state where fear, reasonable or unreasonable, is diminished or reduced to manageable proportions; a state of affairs, where the entire society maintains confident in the institutions that bind them, a state where man can confidently seek and find his due place in the society.

Unity does not mean uniformity. Unity implies that individual situations are not condemned to repeat themselves from generation to generation within a united policy.

Political unity does not mean that differences cease to exist. Rather, it means that differences are recognized and accommodated to the satisfaction of all concerned. Political unity means that both privilege and handicaps are not automatic.

Whenever we consider the word, unity, we must always bear in mind that there are two forms of unity: unity of Jonah inside the belly of the whale and the unity of marriage, when differences come together to bring forth increase.

The biggest obstacle to unity is that which is commonly known and referred to as selfishness; personal interest as against general interest. Suffice it to say that selfishness will weaken or completely destroy the chord of unity which binds us together as a people. It has been said and I believe it is true that development affects traditional, political, social and economic systems. In Etche, we have tried to prove the opposite. We, as a people, are adept at making only minor alterations and slight modifications.

We steadfastly refuse to make fundamental changes. We strive obsessively to fit modern ideals into traditional systems. Where no traditional system exists, we refuse to be daunted and simply manufacture tradition. We design progressive plans only to stuff them into a rigid reactionary polity.

Politicians find it very difficult to raise the rigid discipline and strict accountability which a well articulated ideology imposes both on the leader and the led. Politicians find selfish argument a useful way of easing pressure when assaulted by superior ideas.

Hitherto, the hurdles on our path to political unity have always been placed by the few with vested interests. These are people with selfish and inordinate ambition for power and wealth, men who fear losing their positions and privileges, men who care more for self than for Etche people and their common good. The time has come to take leave of these false prophets in our midst. We must now turn our backs and shun these leaders who have neither the aptitude nor the interest in articulating a political philosophy.

As a people, we must face realities squarely and decide what we want. If we believe in political unity, then we must accept that our survival can only be through unity. Without unity we will perish. Then we must be prepared to approach the issue of unity and brotherly solidarity realistically, selflessly, fearlessly and with a singularity of purpose. We must overcome old prejudices, entrench genuine interests so that we can banish the regime of insecurity.

ENDING THE POLITICS OF DISUNITY
Disunity is a danger that the people of this land can no longer endure. Disunity has led to waste of all the noble dreams of our founding fathers. It has nullified all our efforts at communal reconstruction. Disunity has led us into political crisis and has also destroyed our peace.

The consequences of disunity are too terrible to contemplate and too obvious to require any further demonstration. Disunity denied us the opportunity of producing a senator, minister and governor in a country were we are *bonafide* citizens. The legalized political barbarism of the contemporary Etche situation is the fruit of political disunity.

The only way to banish disunity is to unite; there is no other way. I have said many times, and shall continue to say so until I am heard, that the problem with Etche is not economic, social, and cultural. The problem with Etche is political disunity.

It is politics that distorts everything and it is politics by an internal dialectic that renders everything we touch putrid and poisonous. It is even politics that distorts our view of politics. Often times in our various wards, we do not find the politician insulted, castigated and pilloried, yet politics remains the noblest arena for public service. Some of our politicians are the most honourable in the land. We have, sooner or later, to face the fact that our problems are too deep rooted to be solved by slogans and escape-goats.

We all know that the pattern of Nigerian politics since the inception of the Fourth Republic in 1999 has been that of imposition and intimidation. Etche people have not within this period truly exercised their sovereign rights in deciding who should represent them. This persistent imbalance, whenever perceived by those not favoured by it, remains a source of provocation and a threat to peace.

To achieve unity and progress, we have to urgently redefine, for ourselves, the best method to adopt in choosing our representatives: Councillors, members of House of Assembly, Local Government Chairmen, Members of House of representatives, Senators, and other desired elective positions.

In so doing, we must articulate what the basic assumptions are; what the recognizable and acceptable component units, the irreducible factors, norms, institutions and above all, what the purposes are. This calls for a free open communal dialogue.

Those who must lead Etche people must first free themselves from all that is primitive and primordial in thought, word and deed. They must appreciate that societies do not grow overnight as mushroom or by miracle. Developed societies are the result of vision, commitment, selfless sacrifice by men and women who believe in the cause of the nation.

Our future leaders must therefore reinforce *'Cheta Ala Etche, Mee Ya Nma'* from the realms of rhetoric and fix it resolutely in the concrete domain of action. We must realize that Etche is too precious, too large, and complicated, that she cannot be entrusted to puny minds or minds atrophied by prejudice or any form of bigotry.

Let us not be bogged down by an egocentric defense of words; words are a mere vehicle, at best inadequate, for conveying sense. Action is what concretizes sense as words merely elaborate vision. In the Etche situation, the beginning of all wisdom is the establishment of peace within the confines of our communal and political life.

We are all Etche people; the business of our people is the business of all. It is pertinent that I conclude this chapter with the following quotations:

(a) *The biggest disease today is not leprosy or tuberculosis, but rather the feeling of being*

unwanted, uncared for and deserted by everybody. The greatest evil is the lack of love and charity, the terrible indifference towards one's neighbour who lives at the roadside assaulted by exploitation, corruption, poverty and disease.
- Mother Theresa of India

(b) *Nothing will happen in our nation, in our society, which did not first happen in our minds. If wrong is rampant, if indiscipline is rife, if corruption is the order of the day, we have to search our individual minds for that is where it all starts.*
- Late Justice Chukwudifu Oputa
Former Judge of the Supreme Court of Nigeria

Let us always remember that there is only one price which is too great to pay for peace and harmony, self respect. This is the dream we have been asked to transform into reality. This is the honour we have been called upon to share. This is the noble heritage I implore all to leave to our posterity.

I feel proud that I come from Etche. Many ethnic nationalities in Rivers State do not boast of the expanse of land and natural resources we have in Etche. I see an Etche that would be vibrant and united in diversity. I see a brighter tomorrow which, hitherto, had been a hope for a greater glory of Etche. I am inspired with strength and convinced that no problem is insurmountable; that there are always solutions to everything; that all our beloved land needs is the habit of togetherness.

SECTION THREE

THE PULSE OF DEVELOPMENT

---◆--------◆---

*Education is the most powerful
weapon which you can use to change the world*

-Nelson Mandela

---◆--------◆---

CHAPTER TEN

IT TAKES EDUCATION

Until something changes within you, nothing changes around you. Every change begins from within. Without a change within, there can never be a change without.

-Dr. David Oyedepo

There cannot be development and transformation in Etcheland without qualitative education. People who are addicted to the pursuit of knowledge are always naturally agents of change and pioneers. It's been more than 20 years since I finished my secondary school education at County Grammar School Ikwerre/Etche and more than 12 years that I left Rivers University of Science and Technology and later University of Port Harcourt. When I look back, I can confidently say that, I am what I am today, by the power of education. The education that I acquired has effectively set me up for the future. I can confidently move into the future, because I know that I have acquired what it takes to confront it.

Moreover, having been excellently equipped by the power of education, I can meaningful make my contribution in any circle I find myself. Education has correctly positioned me in my generation to be a contributor, instead of a consumer. Education has fortified my mind against any challenge I will encounter in the future.

In my opinion, nothing empowers like education. To be educated is to be empowered; and to be uneducated is to be disempowered. Education is the gateway for societal development and the cure for our backwardness as a people.

The first step towards introducing sustainable development in Etche ethnic nationality is to embrace and pursue quality education. Education is the key factor to man's success in the race of life. Every development is traceable to education in our quest for a change of position.

Etcheland can only be developed when its people get properly educated. Our backwardness is rooted in lack of education. Because we lack education, we are deformed and because we are deformed, we impede development. If there must be a change, then we must be properly informed. Being informed is not just knowing something; it involves possessing a working knowledge of that thing.

Education can radically change the life of an individual. And when our life is changed, our society will change. Nothing is more effective in the quest to achieve development than commitment to education. The improvement that takes place in a transformed society is

How we got here

The Etche man's handicap in acquiring formal education was caused by three major factors. These are traditional, parental attitude and the environmental factors.

Traditional Factor

The level of intelligence of the people of Etche is in no way inferior to that of their counterparts elsewhere. The academic brilliance of many Etche young men and women who had the opportunity proves this beyond all reasonable doubt.

Unlike most communities which had the cause to struggle for survival through the medium of education, the lot of the Etche man was that of complete satisfaction in the midst of abundant food.

The primary reason why people go to school is to acquire education as a means of livelihood. Education gives them the background to be employed and acquire skills from which they feed themselves and cater for their children and families.

The Etche man felt that he has already been abundantly provided with the basic needs of life. Every adult member thought that he had the easy means of securing regular meals and clothes for himself. To the conservative Etche family, education was only for the lazy and the landless. Therefore, there was no cogent reason for pursuing western education.

Parental Attitude Factor

It is important to stress the influence of the parent against educational advancement in Etche. Rather than allowing the *'Nwa di ala'* go to school, the Etche man gave all the opportunity to his servants; the strangers he had haboured. It was the children of the landless who attended the early schools in Etche.

Although traditions die hard, yet, with time, they change and are transformed and modernized. When the land was increasingly over cultivated and yields became lesser by the season, many felt the need for alternative source of livelihood. Traditional antagonism against going to school mellowed down. But parental attitude remained unbending in opposition of children going to school.

The Etche parent defiantly proffered three strong reasons why the school was not an ideal place for his children. He did not like the idea of his children rubbing shoulders with strangers whose background he very much suspected.

Furthermore, the father required the children to help him in farm-work. Here, traditional and parental attitude found meeting ground in effectively preventing the Etche child from going to school, to acquire formal education early enough, like his counterparts elsewhere.

The third reason was the misplaced sympathy and attachment which the parent, especially the mother, nursed for the children. Etche people lacked everything but food. Their children ate any time they wanted.

Only the parent who could not afford to provide food for the child whenever the child wanted to eat would push the child into the '*world of starvation*', in reference to the hours spent at school. Those who allowed their children to experience such deprivation sent them to school with large cooked yam soaked in oil and vegetables.

The Environmental factor

The fourth reason for the backwardness of Etche people in the field of education was lack of educational facility. By the early 50's, only two primary schools with standard six existed in the three native administration areas of Etche. These were: Saint Luke's Omuma, 1950, which was then generally called Omuma Central School, Eberi Omuma and Saint Mathias School, Egwi/Okomoko. Almost every Etche child who pursued education by the 50's was a graduate of one of the two schools except one studied outside the Etchè kingdom.

There were other primary schools, but they were only standard four schools. The two, premier institutions belonged to the Church Missionary Society of Anglican. Their door however, were left open to all shades of religious groups. It was during the later part of the 50s that more primary schools were upgraded to standard six.

Secondary education was not embraced early in Etche. This affected the people's opportunities for early university or tertiary education. The delay was the late establishment of a secondary school in Etche. Although, the first known school was established in 1916 in Etche, there was no secondary school in the whole of Etche untll 1956 when the Catholic Mission established St. Joseph's Teachers Training College at Umuaturu. This neglect on the part of the missions and government made the hunger for secondary education in Etche land difficult to be assuaged.

Another reason was the much interest shown by Etche sons and daughters in primary school teaching job. Most of the early beneficiaries of primary education in Etche took to teaching. Rather than pursue secondary education, they received teaching orientation in the Pupils Teachers College (PTC) and Teachers College (TC) programmes. This limited progression of the earliest beneficiaries of primary education to follow secondary school education. The situation therefore resulted in lopsided power development in Etche. There are more people in teaching than other professions. This trend is still on today.

There was also the problem of complacency, culminating in the local champion syndrome. Some of the early beneficiaries of western education felt satisfied with their contemporaries who did not go to school. Rather than look outside to compete with colleagues from other lands they limited themselves to Etche and, therefore saw little need in going further.

OUR PREDICAMENT
John F. Kennedy said: "For time and the world do not stand still. Change is the law of life. And those who look only to the past or the present are certain to miss the future." Etche people are seriously backward in terms of manpower, political and economic development as a result of poor educational history. We became stagnated, confused and confounded as a people. Our future is uncertain and unpredictable. Consequently, our children's experience are in total dilemma and despondency. Our beloved land is in complete disarray as a result of violence and self-inflicted crisis. With due respect to our founding fathers and those who are still struggling to improve the standard of Etche nation, I regret to say that the maxim; *"Cheta Ala Etche, Me Ya Nma"* has been reduced to *"Cheta Ala Etche, Me Ya Njo"*. What a shame! What a disappointment!

For the purpose of diagnosis and emphasis, I will like to identify the various stages and cadres of our backwardness as a people.

MANPOWER SHORTAGE

It is not difficult to discover that Etche people are in acute shortage of professionals. A research I conducted in 2007 revealed that the number of professionals among Etche people is less than ten percent of the entire population. Ninety percent are uneducated and unskilled people, who are struggling to survive.

Professionalism is the end product of education. The long years of educational neglect has resulted in the shortage of professionals today. The power and pride of every nation are dependent on the number of professionals they parade. Etche lacks the dignified representation of certain caliber of professionals.

The question is, how many of the following professionals do we parade in Etcheland: lawyers, bankers, engineers, doctors, architects, lecturers, pilots, clergymen, industrialists, scientists etc? It is the number of professionals we have that determines how educationally serious we have been as a society.

Having more of these professionals is what projects us as being formidable while having less of them classifies us as weak people in the comity of nations.

Think about this: If about 50% of Etche adult citizens are professionals or skilled, what kind of Etche will we have? A respected Etche! Moreover, we will not only be respected wherever we go to, we will be highly influential, because we have a lot to offer. Education commands undeniable respect and honour, while ignorance attracts rejection and disrespect.

As I move from office to office in the course of my business and as we take stock on the happenings in the political and economic field of this great nation, we can scarcely count the number of our people who are in key positions in state and federal sectors. These are what lack of education and skilled training have denied us.

There are several communities in Etche that have no single lawyer, doctor, engineer, or architect. So many families have no graduate. Who represents them when they are in need of the services of professionals? They end up hiring the service of an outsider who charges and collects the money they would have used in training one of their own.

COMMUNAL BACKWARDNESS

The story of Etche people is replete with stagnation, under-development, backwardness, ignorance and communal crisis. All of the above mentioned identities are all rooted in educational background. A man can never think or grow beyond what he knows. It is the quantum of knowledge in a man that determines what he does. More knowledge commands positive actions, while less knowledge can only result in less action; in most cases negative action.

Towards the end of 2009, I decided to visit most communities in Etche to ascertain our present level of development and the following are my findings: Several communities in Etche are engaged in communal crises which have resulted in killing of people, burning down of houses, destruction of properties and in some cases, relocation of indigenes to neighbouring villages.

Secondly, so many Etche roads are in deplorable condition. Most of our rural communities have no access road to and fro their farms, especially during rainy season

Thirdly, over 90% of Etche communities are not connected to the national electricity grid. Whatever development and improvement that accompanies power supply has completely been denied them.

Fourthly, there is no federal government presence in the entire Etche land. The only federal road linking Rivers State to Imo State, which passed through Igwuruta-Etche-Ngo -kpala, is in bad shape. Most of the state government-owned companies in Etche have become moribund.

Fifthly, the number of uneducated and unemployed Etche youths is increasing by the day. Most of the youths have taken to crime, drugs, and other vices, which are alien to our tradition as a people. Communal backwardness is caused by educational backwardness. We are here today because of the level of education attained.

Unqualified persons have been forcefully put in position, against the wishes and aspiration of Etche people. It is on record that most people who occupy political offices presently are uneducated and therefore lack the capacity to lead. They occupy political offices, which they use to deprive the people of the dividend of democracy.

POLITICAL BACKWARDNESS

We have not faired better politically. In fact, the story of our political experience has been that of retrogration. Since the inception of the present Fourth Republic in 1999, we have not made any significant improvement.

Politics is generally regarded as an instrument of liberation and empowerment. Unfortunately, ours has been the use of power to intimidate, divide and destroy the people. Those who are privileged to hold political power, have abused the privilege by using it as if it was their right. In order to protect their political position, they employed violence and divide and rule tactics.

In our society, we now have a situation where, instead of the electorate to choose their representatives, it is the representatives that choose their voters. They now choose who votes, and who should not vote in an election. It is sad to say that political leaders, who are expected to be agents of peace and unity, have become agents of violence and destruction. It is on record that our political leaders use intimidation and violence to scare the people from exercising their constitutional rights. What a shame?

Our political backwardness has equally affected our political representation among other ethnic groups within the state and federal government. Because we produce weak and unprepared leaders, they end up giving us bad representation wherever they are. Their voices are never heard in support of Etche people. Advocacy and vibrancy have been relegated to the back burner. They lack the political will to draw the attention of the world to the deplorable and sorry state of Etche people. This may be as a result of selection and not election.

ECONOMIC BACKWARDNESS
Etche does not have influential and well established multi millionaires not to talk of billionaires.

On the other hand, majority of our people are still peasant farmers and petty traders. Over 90% of our people are struggling to survive. Though we have abundant land for agriculture, we are still engaged in hand-to-mouth-farming and not commercial agriculture. This is because we don't have the wherewithal to acquire the multi-million naira equipment required for such enterprise. It is a surprise to note that Etche people, who claim to have all the food in the world before now, which discouraged their children from going to school, are unable to feed them today. What a tragedy!

Based on existing data and statistics and the living standard of people, majority of Etche people are poor, and they live below poverty line. But thank God, we now have a generation of people who want to change and project the dreams of Etche people.

CHAPTER ELEVEN

STRUGGLE TOWARDS EXCELLENCE

Excellence is an art won by training and habitation. We do not act rightly because we have virtue or excellence, but we rather have these because we have acted rightly. We are what we repeatedly do. Excellence, then, is not act but a habit.

-Aristotle

Education is an ornament in prosperity and a refuge in adversity. Education is the best provision for development. Absolute commitment towards the pursuit of mass education is the only solution to the state of our underdevelopment. If we desire to project our future, then we must develop love for education. We must become hungry and desperate to acquire education.

In projecting the Next Etche Development Project ((NEDEP), education of our people is a key factor. Education prepares our people for the project. The education of our people is the fundamental tool with which we can use to speedily develop Etche kingdom.

I consider education as a system of well organized deciminated information that is intended to influence our thoughts and actions for better society. It is the force that rules the world. Education is about building the capacity required to pursue a project. For example, if you want to build a solid mansion, what process would you follow? Will you just call the builder to dig a foundation and commence the laying of blocks? Not at all. First, you are required to sit down with an architect and come up with a building design. Secondly, you will cost the project and also determine if you have the money needed to finish the building during the stipulated time frame. Thirdly, you will negotiate and agree with the civil engineer before awarding the contract. It is only when you are done with all these, that you will commence the project.

The plans that precedes building a mansion can be compared to acquiring education. Education is the foundation required to promote The Next Etche Development Project. Without adequate education, our dream will be unfulfilled.

Education is whatever information, news, teaching, knowledge and personal experiences that will empower Etche people to pursue the project of developing Etche kingdom. It is the understanding of what we must do and how we should do it. Education is the gathering of the details required before launching out. We also need continuous education to sustain the project. Education will take us to the top; it will also keep us at the top. Education will bring success, it will sustain the success.

Education is like reading the design, and drawing about locations and places on a map before proceeding on a journey. If you are to travel to an unknown destination, you are required to first study the map. This will help you know the locations and places when you arrive there. Projecting the Next Etche Development Project(NEDEP) is our destination; the advance study of map is the acquisition of the needed education to actualize the project.

Education is like farming tools, equipment and seeds. Any farmer who goes to the farm without tools and seed will not have anything to reap during the harvesting season. He will end up in hunger and frustration. In fact, he is a foolish and confused farmer. Education is like farming implements and seeds required to achieve our project. If we do not have the relevant tools and seeds, we may end up as failures

THE POWER OF EDUCATION
There is an incredible power in Education. Nothing transforms like knowledge. To be informed is to be transformed; and to be uninformed is to be deformed. Education is our advancement and the solution for all our frustration as a people. Education has incredible power - the transformation power. In the following lines, I will take you through six powers of education in the life of a people, especially our people. We will be discussing what

education can do specifically for us as a people who are on transition to the next level of development.

EDUCATION BREEDS PROFESSIONALS

The huge gap of inadequate professionals in Etche created by educational negligence can only be filled by a new awareness for educational pursuit. Education is the only means by which we can increase the number of professionals that we will parade in the comity of nations.

Please, this is very important. Education will increase the number of the professionals we parade. The professionals will increase our capacity to receive more from the system. The rule of life is capacity before position. We cannot occupy the position that we have no capacity for.

The size of what you carry is determined by your weight or capacity, the position that you occupy is determined by your knowledge and expertise. Gone are the days when ignorant people are put in a position of trust. In today's business world, it is experts that call the short. What education does is to turn you to an expert. If Etche people want to increase the number of professional in their midst in the next ten years, then we must seriously increase the number of our youths in school. Remember, the time we spend in education is not time wasted, rather it is time invested

EDUCATION CREATES WEALTH
Wealth creation is activated through the power of ideas. What education does to a man is to improve or sharpen his ability to think. Education enhances your reasoning ability; it secures ideas, while ideas create wealth.

Therefore, if you are not properly educated, you can not be a good thinker, and if you are not a good thinker, you will never have good ideas. Without good ideas, you will remain poor.

The excruciating pain of poverty can only be cheaply broken through the power of education. Education is the act of sharpening the brain. It is the sharpening of the brain that commands success. At the root of every gain is the use of the brain. It is brain work that makes things work. Wealth is indeed a product of man's ability to think.

EDUCATION PROVIDES LEADERSHIP
Quality leadership is determined by quality education. On the other hand, poor leadership is determined by poor education. There is a proverb in Etche that says: *"Onye Ishi duru Onye ishi, we nnam ga idaba nime Olulu"* (if a blind man leads a blind man, they will fall into the ditch). This is perfectly true about life. We cannot grow beyond the quality of our leadership. Quality leadership is determined by quality education.

Even though a school of thought has argued that education does not guarantee wisdom for leadership, I believe that such cases where the uneducated lead very well are an exception, they are not too many in today's world. People, all over the world, depend on the educated for both political, economic and traditional leadership.

I believe that time has come when our political office holders must not be elected if they are not graduates of higher institutions. Our councilors must be graduates to be elected. We must go beyond the constitutional requirement of secondary school certificate. Secondary school knowledge is no longer relevant in today's changing world. We need higher knowledge in order to meet up with the challenges we are facing as a people.

Also, our traditional rulers and chiefs must know how to read and write before they are to lead our communities. The assignment and function of chiefs have gone beyond settling internal communal disputes. They are expected to become agents of communal transformation. They ought to provide effective leadership that will attract development to their various domains.

Community development committee (CDC) leaders must all be educated. This will enhance their ability to be successful in their primary assignment of community development.

I believe that Etche people deserve effective leadership. We need frontline leaders at this point of our odyssey. This dream can only be realized when more people become educated.

EDUCATION LEADS TO DEVELOPMENT
Education cannot leave you the same way it found you. Education commands change. What educated people do is to champion development.

EDUCATION DETERMINES SPEED
The speed of development in Etche will be determined by the quality of information at our disposal and the level of insight with which we are operating. We can not go beyond the information at our disposal.

The brighter we see, the faster we go, the more informed we are, the faster we develop Etche. The brightness of light in your car determines your speed at night. If the brightness of your car light is poor, and you attempt speed, you have signed in for fatal accident. You may not only loose the vehicle, you will loose your life.

Education is light. What light is to a car in the night is what education is to development. It determines our speed of accomplishment.

AVENUES FOR EDUCATION
We live in a changing world. So you have to keep pace with current knowledge. If the information at your disposal is obsolete, then it cannot produce any meaningful result. I believe that tradition is the worst enemy of civilization, because it has no regard for current knowledge.

We are living in an age where knowledge is exploding. Studies have shown that half way point of all human knowledge is located less than ten years ago; that is, man's knowledge has doubled within the past decade. Every 60 seconds, 2000 typewritten pages are added to man's knowledge and the materials produced every 24 hours takes one person 5 years to read.

If a lawyer or doctor sat down and read the law or medical journals in his field as his full time job, at the end of a year they would be three months behind in their reading. At the moment, we have a computer memory that can assimilate into permanent storage 5 million per second. That is the same as assimilating the entire Bible six times in one second.

The person who thinks he knows everything has a lot to learn! Thomas A. Edison made the comment: *"we do not know one million part of one percent about anything. We do not know what water is; we do not know what electricity is. We do not know what gravity is. We do not know anything about magnetism. We have a lot of hypotheses, but that is not all".* That means we have a lot to know about these things he mentioned. What we know about them now is not enough. Facts are what make one to profit wonderfully, obtain adequate information. What are the avenues of education? Let me share some of them with you.

EDUCATION

Formal education is when you officially or formally enroll for learning in an educational institution. Informal education can be obtained by engaging a private tutor or attending seminars, workshops and other related programs. Both formal and informal education will expand your scope of understanding and increase your capacity to acquire more knowledge.

May be you are not a graduate of higher school now, and you desire to have your doctorate degree, the total number of years it will take you is less than ten years. You can get started now. Informal education also includes listening to tapes, CDs and DVDs; and even learning on the internet. There is no information you cannot find on the internet. Listen to good programmes on radio and television. We are in the age of success, so let us invest. Let us spend time to acquire information, because it will determine the level of development in Etche.

READING

The most effective avenue for knowledge acquisition is reading. Reading makes living successful. Most of the greatest minds in today's world emerged out of a studious life. The quality of information that finds its way into your mind determines the quality of your mind.

Anthony Robins has grown to become a consultant to big corporations such as IBM, the US Army, AT&T, etc, by

reading. By virtue of information, the capacity of his mind has been enormously enlarged. Benjamin Franklin had only two years of formal education, before he branched off to become a printing apprentice.
He taught himself how to read. He read and read until he became more intelligent then the writers of the books he read. He founded a university, built a specialist hospital, and became one of America's foremost philosophers.

Michael Faraday was also an apprentice in a book binding centre. Though uneducated, he taught himself how to read. He spent his money to attend scientific seminars and grew to become an inventor. Nothing dignifies life like light, nothing enhances development like information. So settle down to consciously acquire relevant information through reading.

OBSERVATION
Exposure is the price for exploit. There are a lot to learn from the happenings around you. Every opportunity should provide us with information. We must observe those who are ahead of us. We must learn what made them successful. Sometimes, the best way to learn is not by asking question, but to quietly observe.

In Etche culture, a young girl may necessarily not ask the mother to enroll her in a cooking lesson. If her desire is to know how to cook, all she needs to do is to observe the mother closely while she is preparing the meal. As she is assisting the mother, she will naturally understand how to cook a meal.

There is no point discovering or re-inventing our knowledge, since nothing is new under the sun. Let us borrow the knowledge that made others what they are.

DESPERATELY PURSUE EDUCATION

Any hunter who desires to eat meat must go for hunting. Animals do not surrender or run to the hunter to be killed. It is the responsibility of the hunter to search, chase, shoot and catch the animal. It is only when the hunter has caught the animal that he can sit down and enjoy the meat. Any hunter, who decides to wait for an animal to run to him without a search and chase, will wait forever in hunger. Likewise, information acquired through education does not jump on people; you search for it. If we want to enjoy the benefits of information and become a developed society, we must desperately pursue education.

If we must reclaim the dream of placing Etche on the world map, then we must kickstart a process of mass education in Etche land. If an Etche man and woman must make impact in their lives, then we must develop insatiable hunger for more insight in our professions.

A wise man said, and I totally agree with him: "you will be the same that you are this year in five years time, except for two things the books you read and the people with who you walk." A time will come when the things we know will no longer be relevant to the needs of the people around us.

No matter our profession or career, without relevant knowledge, we don't have a future. We cannot become a developed society by wishing. We only become one by learning what it takes to project our agenda.

It has been proved beyond reasonable doubt that committed readers are those who become great leaders. You cannot lead anyone if you don't see ahead. Dedicated readers and knowledge hunters are the people that become great leaders. Remember, common sense, at its best, will only produce common results.

Henry Ford said: "Anyone who stops learning is old, either at twenty or eighty. Anyone who keeps learning stays young. The greatest thing in life is to keep your mind young". That is to keep one's mind open to new insight and knowledge that will help in generating solution to bugging issues in Etche.

Education demands discipline, as it does not jump on people. It is only available to explorers. It is a product of intelligent search. Etche people must wake up to this new consciousness. You, in particular, the reader of this book, must realize that the only way you can join in this revolution of projecting The Etche Development Agenda is to be educated. If you are already educated, there is room for constant improvement. There is never enough knowledge, you can know more.

SECTION FOUR

ETCHE AND ITS ECONOMY

*All labour that uplifts humanity
has dignity and importance
and should be undertaken
with painstaking excellence*

Dr. Martin Luther King Jr.

CHAPTER TWELVE

PREVIEW OF ETCHE
ECONOMIC ACTIVITIES

All labour that uplifts humanity has dignity and importance and should be undertaken with painstaking excellence.

-Dr. Martin Luther King, Jr

There are a wide variety of economic activities taking place in Etche land. It is very well known that land is the source of the wealth of Etche people. The economic life-wire of the people depends on farming and the exploitation of the rich natural resources of the land. Majority of the people make a livelihood on farming, animal husbandry, fishing, forestry, food processing, cottage industry and crafts.

Farming is the main economic activity of the people. Over 80% percent of the population is engaged in it. There is no town or village where farming is not practiced. The vegetation characteristics of the area sustain a large number of crops; hence the area is regarded as the food basket of Rivers State. Among the crops planted are cassava, yam, maize, cocoyam, melon, pumpkin, pepper, garden egg, sugar cane, plantain, okro and a host of and streams, fishing activities are carried out. These areas include: Obibi, Umuelechi, Umuokurukpuo Chokocho, Igbo, Egwi Nihi, Odufor, Akpoku, Isu, Ogida, Owu, Ndadsi, Obite, Afara, Akwa, Mba, Umuanyagu, Okoroagu, Odagwa and others. There are part-time fishermen also. About 10% of the population is engaged in this occupation.

Hunting is also substantially undertaken. It could be done on an individual basis or as a group activity in the day or night. The main games hunted include: antelope, grass cutter, porcupine, pigs, leopard, etc. Apart from hunting, trapping is also employed to catch games.

Various forms of animal husbandry are carried out in various parts of Etcheland both to supplement household protein and for commercial purposes. Goats, pigs and sheep are reared in commercial quantities. Pigs are kept on a small scale basis relative to goats and sheep. Most homes in Etche also keep poultry for both commercial and domestic uses.

In Etche, palm wine is tapped from raffia palm. Raffia palms grow naturally along river banks and are scattered in the mangrove forest. Some are also planted within the villages and / or river banks. About 8% of the population is actively engaged in this activity. People from neighbouring ethnic communities, especially the Ogonis, are actively involved in palm wine tapping. This occupation thrives in villages and towns living near the rivers and stream as in fishing.

TRADITIONAL INDUSTRIES IN ETCHE
The processing of certain agricultural produce is also carried out in commercial quantities like garri, which is a staple food in Nigeria. Traditional method is used.

Attempts to introduce modern method at Umuechem and Isu have not taken deep root. To process garri, cassava is peeled and grinded into paste by the use of machine. It is then bagged and de-watered to form hard lumps which are sieved and fried to produce the garri. A typical household processes about 2 to 4 bags of garri a week which are sold in the numerous local markets that abound in the area.

Palm oil, which is used for cooking by virtually every house hold in Etche, is processed from ripe palm fruits. Traditional methods are used to extract oil. The fruits are boiled, pounded into pulps and water poured in; the floating oil is skillfully scooped from the water and heated to separate the oil from impurities. The extraction of palm oil results in the joint supply of palm oil and palm kernel oil (Manuaku).

Local crafts also abound in Etche. These include cloth weaving, mat and bag making, fishing traps etc. These activities are not very widespread and are faced with near extinction, perhaps owing to their low income yield and lack of interest by the younger generation.

MODERN INDUSTRIES IN ETCHE

Modern industries referred to here are those industries brought into the area from outside. The earliest known ones are the oil mills established at Umuaturu in 1945, Chokocho in 1951 and Eberi, Omuma, in about 1956. These were followed by the establishment of Abara Rubber Estate by the Eastern Nigeria Development Corporation (ENDC) in 1963. Other plantations were established at Umuoye, Odagwa and Akwa in 1965. Because of the viability of these plantations, Delta Rubber Company was established at Umuanyagu/Okomoko to produce rubber crumbs for export and to feed local industries.

Following a geographical survey of some parts of Etche in 1978, Risonpaim Nucleus Estate was established in 1980. It acquired a large expanse of land at Isu, Ogida, Egbu, Ozuzu, and Ihie. Another modern industry is FAMAP Company that grew citrus and pineapples as well as other fruits. It is worthy of mention that most of these modern industries have gone moribund.

THE OIL INDUSTRY

Oil exploration is at the apex of economic activities in Etche. The first discovery of mineral oil in Etche land was in 1956 at Umuechem, although drilling commenced in 1958. This was followed by other discoveries at Umuebulu and Odagwa in 1962, Chokota and Ikwerrengwo in 1972

(National Population Census Historical Data, Etche Division 1973). Further oil deposit discoveries were made at Abara in 1974, Isu in 1979, Akpoku, Mba, Obuo and Umuoye in 1980, Okoroagu in 1979 and others.

Today, statistical evidence shows that Etche ranks second and fourth in the production of crude oil and gas respectively in Rivers State.

ETCHE ECONOMIC CHALLENGES

The destiny of Etche people is in their hands. What we make out of it is primarily our responsibility. There has never been any social development without confronting challenges. Our case is not an exception. We have several challenges which I believe have become our limitation. Let us identify some of the challenges and the way out.

Manpower or Professional Challenge

We lack the manpower or the professionalism required to create a robust economy in Etcheland. Manpower development is the principal tool for restructuring the economic life of a people. It is true that there are lots of artisans such as mechanics, welders, carpenters, bicycle repairers, photographers and masons. Etche has also produced medical doctors, lawyers, engineers and career civil and public servants.

However, the number is still not sufficient to attract the development we have long desired. The greater the number of manpower and professionals we have, the greater the development they will attract. Like I said in Chapter One, we need to declare state of emergency in the education sector in Etche land. Organized and concerted effort should be put in place to ensure that Etche sons and daughters are either formally educated, or assisted to acquire technical skills.

Technological Challenge

The Etche economy is predominantly rural and agrigarian. It is technologically deficient. This has hindered the transformation of this traditional economy into a modern one. It has also encumbered the growth and development of not only the Etche people but the entire society.

Farming in this modern world has gone beyond the use of knife and hoe for cultivation. It requires the use of modern equipment such as tractors, which will reduce the number of manpower and hours spent cultivating, harvesting and processing farm proceeds.

Unavailability of technology has also prevented us from industrializing agriculture in Etche. We are still at the level of hand-to-mouth agricultural businesses.

Tenant Companies' Challenge

Etche serves as host to a few industries. The penetration of these modern industries such as SPDC, Risonpalm Nig. Ltd. and Delta Rubber Company has not positively

I believe that this is primarily due to the predatory nature of their operations. In fact, these companies engage in parasitical accumulation and siphoning the surplus of the area to serve their mother countries, as in the case of SPDC, to enrich and develop other parts of Nigeria

In general, there is unequal exchange in the relationship between Etche ethnic nationality and these infiltrators. These firms have cornered virtually all the benefits arising from their operations, leaving little or nothing in return. For example, the massive de-peasantisation of Etche people occasioned by the primitive acquisition of land by Risonpaim, Delta Rubber and SPDC, has intensified the problems of land, hunger, land disputes and penury.

Government Challenge
Another major challenge militating against the economic development of Etche is the neglect by federal and state governments. The Federal and state governments have been unkind to Etche in terms of provision of supportive infrastructure. The distribution of its largesse among its constituent units and people of the state has continued to be inequitable. Much of the state resources have been cornered by other ethnic groups whose sons and daughters are placed in different strategic positions in the economy. Etche has not had the blessing of controlling any part of Rivers or Nigerian economy, not even controlling her own resources. This has stifled the growth of Etche people and adversely affected their economy.

Patriotism Challenge

Apart from the above exogenous influences, Etche has endogenous inhibiting factors. There is the lack of spirit of enterprise and ingenuity among some Etche people. Most Etche sons and daughters are known to have frittered away their opportunities to grow into big-time businessmen and politicians because of the myopia of not looking far into the future and their high propensity to live in premating grandiosity.

Besides, there are also the problems of pettiness and jealousy. A prosperous Etche son or daughter faces the challenge of being extinguished in his or her prime as a result of envy and pettiness. Patriotism to Etche seems to be lacking among some of the people. Some people have the narrow mindedness of trying to be the only tree in forest

CHAPTER THIRTEEN

INSTITUTIONALIZING
PRODUCTIVITY

Do not pray for easy lives. Pray to be strong men.

-J.F Kennedy

G rowing up in my rural community, Egwi, in Etche Local Government Area, I had my fair participation in the day to day economic occupation of our people which was primarily designed for just survival and not empowerment. I went to the farm with my parents as a young boy. I joined some hired daily labourers to clear the bush. After the cleared bush is properly dried, it is set on fire. Then the clearance and cultivation began as the rain was expected to wet the land. I also participated in the weeding of the farm.

Within three to four months of cultivation, some of the crops were ready for harvesting. These crops were maize, pumpkin and vegetable. Then others following suit, namely ; yam and cassava, three leave yam, cocoa yam etc. I have also been asked several times to take the products to the market for sale. I have sold them several times as a young man, so I know the commercial value of such products. My primary and secondary school expenses were paid with proceeds from farming. Although my father was a civil servant with the Rivers State Newspaper Cooperation, I can recall that he often said that he makes more money from agricultural products than his salary as a civil servant.

Having participated in and experienced our traditional occupation as a people, I came to the conclusion that such activities will never bring about economic and industrial revolution in Etche land. We can only manage to survive on such activities. They will never bring sustainable empowerment.

I believe that if we must join the economic revolution going on in several communities in Nigeria, then we must change and improve our standard, approach and strategies.

Much is demanded from Etche people, the state and other *dramatis personae* in the Etche economy. There is need for people to turn a new leaf so that the Etche economy can be transformed for the betterment of all. In the remaining lines of this Chapter, I will take you through the standards, approaches and strategies we need to adopt in order to experience economic revolution.

PURPOSE

The first step toward, achieving economic revolution in Etche is to have an economic purpose system. Life is purpose-driven. Man is lifeless without purpose. It is purpose that gives meaning to life. For us to achieve economic revolution in Etche, every Etche son and daughter must have an economic purpose or mission.

If we have mission, we will have motion. It is the sense of mission that ignites the mechanism of motion. Purpose ignites motion; it infuses it with strength and enhances endurance.

Purpose is the foundation of economic revolution. Any society without an economic purpose will remain poor. Every society that has attained economic stability discovered their economic purpose. They know where they are going and are ready to stake their lives for their goal or purpose.

We can't all be politicians, lawyers, doctors or academicians, so let every Etche son and daughter strive to discover his/her purpose and identify with it. Our economic future depends solely on purpose-driven efforts. Our collective purpose is the gateway for economic revolution in Etche land.

PLANNING

Having discovered our economic purpose, the next thing to do is to settle down to plan how to accomplish it. We say between hard work and hard life. Let us stop wishing, and start working. Nothing works until you work it. I believe that there is dignity in labour. Let us stop playing around and start producing. Don't just hang around, looking for who will dole things out to you. If we are not working, we are not only going to become poor, we are signing up to die poor.

PRODUCTIVITY

We will never achieve revolution in Etche without a productive citizenry. It is the input of individuals within a society that results in the overall development of that society. I strongly believe that when you have one rich man in the midst of six poor people, what you have are seven poor people.

Every development rests on the productivity of the society's citizens. A society where only one fifth of its indigenes are working cannot prosper. No matter what our dream as a people are, we can only actualize it by being productive.

When your body is no longer engaged in practical life activities, it begins to disintegrate and decay. The same thing goes for production of goods and services. You need the effective and efficient managing of anything for it to continue to exist, survive and grow positively. When any system is not used, it decays. Activity edifies the body systems, including the mind. It programmes total health to ourselves: "we know where we're going,' but how do we get there?

The planning stage is the stage of thinking through or pondering on how to realize our goals. Planning helps us to locate the essentials that will enhance the accomplishment of our purpose.

Planning can be defined as step-by-step approach towards the accomplishment of a given task. It is a practical approach packaged towards the realization of any set objective. Every purpose is accomplished by wise planning. A wise man said: "Failing to plan is planning to fail'.

HARD WORK
We have too many idle people in Etche. A greater percentage of our people are not gainfully employed. No society can experience economic revolution when a large number of its citizens is not productive. Productivity determines economic revolution.

No one is born rich, neither was anyone born with a three-piece suit and a pair of shoes on. Everybody came into this world stark naked. Nobody carried a purse or cheque book in his hands, when he was born. People arrive here to become what they choose to be; just like some men become rich, others also become poor. Your choice determines what you become.

and vitality for the body. Only productive activities will guarantee the enhancement of our social status and economic evolution.

Production can be defined as the amount of goods produced in any particular activity one engages in life. Some people just waste the whole of their life in unproductive ventures. Watch how much of your time is spent on key activities that bring positive result and success in your life yearly. You will probably discover that the things that occupy about 60% of your time do not add any positive value to your life. When you carry out an overview assessment and evaluation of your last year's performance, can you regard your productivity proper to be 80%? If you are truthful to yourself, you may need to re-order your life activities generally or change environment and job to the appropriate priorities and direction.

TIME MANAGEMENT
I would define time management simply as "being able to and organize the control of your time and work" rather than allowing them to control you. Time is money and it is an irreplaceable asset.

We can only achieve our plan and goals within a time frame. If you are not conscious of your time, you will never be an achiever.
We need to reorder and re-program our daily schedules, if we are to bring economic revolution in Etche land.

Let us examine these three questions to help us understand the importance of time:

- How do you establish that a commodity is essential, precious or valuable?

- Now, what is the most valuable commodity you possess today?

The most valuable commodity we all have in the same quantity and measure is TIME. This is because:-
Time is an infinite, scarce commodity. Time cannot be stored. It is impossible to increase time. The passage of time is constant and time cannot be borrowed, leased or lent. Time is irreversible though redeemable.

Time is life. Time is a valuable capital or asset. Time is more valuable than money. In fact, time is money.

Successful time management shows you how to:
- Gain a better perspective of pending activities and priorities.
- Identify more opportunity to be creative (taking the initiative instead of reacting).
- Deal with, reduce and avoid stress.
- Gain more leisure i.e. create more time for your family, friends and yourself.
- Consistently and systematically attain your goals, so that your life can make meaning and also have a sense of direction.

There is a time for everything. There is an English proverb which says: Take time to work, it is the price of success. Take time to think, it is the source of power. Take time to play, it is the secret of perpetual youth. Take time to read and study, it is the fountain of wisdom. Take time to be friendly, it is the road to happiness. Take time to love, it is the joy of life. Take time to laugh, it is the music of the soul. Each time you do the right thing at the wrong time, you get the wrong result. You will only get the right result if you do the right thing at the right time, hence the essence of time management. There is no amount of time spent on doing a wrong thing that can be equated with just spending appropriate time doing the right things at the right time.

When you notice you have been on the wrong track, try and summon courage to make a u-turn because genuine effort expended timely will produce the expected results.

The New Economy Globalization

Some people may prefer to ignore globalization, rather than embrace it wholeheartedly. We cannot ignore it, because the effect of doing so is detrimental to our progress. In order to bridge the huge gap between developed people and ourselves, we must embrace the positive aspects of globalization.

Globalization is the way forward; it is the environment in which international interaction takes place both now and in the future. It is already taking root in several areas of the economy including productivity, communications and advanced technology. We have nothing to fear in the national race, because our approach and message is timely; the Etche struggle is national in its essence and applications. Our vision for Etche is all-encompassing in its concept, excellence and competitiveness.

Adopting a national stance in economics, politics, tradition and enlightenment brought innumerable benefits to Etche people in the past, and can do so once again under the umbrella of globalization. If we intelligently embrace globalization, we can enjoy our rightful share of the world's riches. Refuse it and we remain in the dark.

While reviewing the world's economic history, one can see the two distinct features: the 'farming age' and the 'industrial age'. However, the last two decades have seen the emergence of a third economic age, dubbed by some as the 'information age'. This age consists of a closely-knit global economy that covers most fields and may therefore also be called the 'age of globalization'. Since this age' requires extremely fast responses and depends on highly sophisticated technologies, it has also been called the 'age of technology'. It is, in fact, a kind of economy that thrives on knowledge and creative ideas, it may therefore, be given a fourth name: the 'age of creative minds'. Let us hope they do not invent any more names to confuse matters further!

Whatever you call it, just as manufacturing did not replace farming, the information technological economy will not replace the industrial economy. As a matter of fact, the Industrial Revolution played a key role in developing agriculture, while the new information technologies have played a similar role in boosting industry.

The importance of the Info Tech economy is therefore not restricted to its intrinsic value as an independent sector, but encompasses its ability to energize agriculture, industry and services; as well as to boost their performance, reduce their costs, open new development horizons and create opportunities these economies cannot generate on their own.

If the desired goal is achieved, we will no longer be talking about a 'new' and 'old' economy, but about a new Info Tech economy. These complement each other, bringing in a new age of 'global' economy from which we ought to benefit. Embracing this will allow us to make up for the opportunities we lost during the industrial revolution.

SECTION FIVE

THE GOD FACTOR

Living in rebellion against the purpose of God describes why people could be suffering in the midst of huge natural, human and material resources which God has provided for man to make living meaningful.

Rt. Rev Okechukwu P. Nwala

CHAPTER FOURTEEN

WHERE DOES GOD COME IN?

When we do what we can, God will do what we can't

-John Mason

John Mason said: "Christian graces are like perfumes; the more they are pressed, the sweeter they smell; like stars that shine brightest in the dark; like trees, the more they are shaken, the deeper root they take, and the more fruit they bear".

The acquisition of formal education is not enough to accelerate transformation and development in society. In preparing a tasty meal, several ingredients will be required to meet the target. Likewise, there are other necessary ingredients without which a complete transformation will never occur. In Etche kingdom, we will need the addition of something more superior than education.

Quality education will produce intellectuals but may not necessarily produce intelligent people. Intellectuals are people taught by men, while intelligent people are taught by God. Intellectualism is the end product of academics, while being intelligent and possessing wisdom are the end products of Christianity. Therefore, we need the combination of intellectualism and intelligence to reconstruct Etche nation.

The founder of Christianity, Jesus Christ, said in his mission statement: *"The spirit of the Lord is upon me, because he hath anointed me to preach the gospel to the poor; he hath sent me to heal the broken-hearted, to preach deliverance to the captives, and recovering of sight to the blind, to set at liberty them that are bruised"* (Luke 4:18).

Christianity is a divine program for the emancipation and empowerment of a people under bondage. It is a heavenly package for the deliverance and liberation of a nation under captivity. It brings freedom to prisoners.

Christianity is a spiritual weapon designed by God to destroy every instrument of oppression and intimidation. It terminates the forces of evil over a people. Christianity is a dynamic power that dominates every occultic power that is manipulating the destiny of a people. It corrects the errors of yester-years and re-positions the people for the future
Christianity is a spiritual instrument created to discover all political, social, traditional, economic problems of people

and proffer workable solutions to all the problems. Christianity is the pathway to social transformation and success. Following God guarantees development and victory. According to history, people who have been under bondage for years sought the help of God, and Immediately God stepped in, there was a total turn around. This has been the pattern all through Bible and modern history as exemplified by the following nations.

THE NATION OF ISRAEL

The people of Israel were under captivity and slavery in Egypt for about four hundred and thirty years. When they could not bear it any more, the Bible recorded in Exodus 2:23 and 24: *"...and the children of Israel sighed by reason of the bondage, and they cried, and their cry came up unto God by reason of the bondage, and God heard their groaning, and God remembered his covenant with Abraham, with Isaac, and with Jacob."*

Reading and studying the account of the ugly experience of the Israelite under captivity in Egypt will help you to better appreciate their predicament. They were not just under captivity, they were slaves. Their captors had no sympathy for them. They had no respect for their life and dignity. They were treated as non-entities, non-stake holders, as Etche people are treated in Nigeria today.

In Exodus 2:24, the scripture recorded: *"And God heard their groaning and God remembered his covenant with*

Abraham, with Isaac, and with Jacob". As soon as they sought God, he responded without delay. Exodus 3: 9, 10 captured God's response. *"Now therefore, behold, the cry of the children of Isreal is come unto me, and I have also seen the oppression where with the Egyptians oppress them; come now therefore, and I will send thee unto pharaoh, that thou mayest bring forth my people, the children of Isreal out of Egypt"*

This mandate given to Moses initiated the deliverance of four hundred and thirty years' slavery experience of the Israelites. It is important to note that deliverance and liberation came their way simply because they called and believed in God Almighty. This shall be the experience of Etche people in Jesus' Name! Please pause reading for a moment and shout seven loud Amen.

Perhaps, I believe that they may have made several attempts to escape, but their captors were too smart and strong for them. When they discovered that they could not liberate themselves, they looked up to God for help. Someone in their midst may have remembered the covenant their forefathers had with God for a better life. When he reminded others about the covenant, they all accepted to seek God's help.

UNITED STATES OF AMERICA
After winning its independence, this new nation's trials were just beginning. The American Revolution had

disrupted the work of the churches. Ministers had become soldiers; laymen had gone out to fight. Other influences also began to tear down the religious fabric so carefully woven during the colonial years.

As a result, the newly formed United States of America began spinning headlong into a moral slump. Drunkenness was epidemic. Of a population of five million people, three hundred thousand were confirmed drunkards. Fifteen Thousand died of alcoholism every year. People were afraid to go out at night for fear of being assaulted. Sensual gratification and the desire for wealth had captured the American scene.

In the month of April 1799, several members of the church manifested great anxiety about the state of religion among the Americans, and expressed a desire that meetings might be appointed for religious conference and special prayer for the outpouring of the Holy Spirit. This request was afterwards made known to the church as a body. They unanimously approved of it, and a conference meeting was accordingly convened.

These people pleaded for another revival like the Great Awakening. Prayer meetings among young people and within the congregation of churches began to spread. Ministers who wanted renewal for their people met for prayer. They believed that revival could come only as a result of fervent prayer.

In 1794, a group of 23 ministers in New England agreed to promote the concert of prayer once again. They signed a circular letter that was sent to every Christian denomination. A year later, this prayer effort became widespread and influential. Would all these prayer efforts have any effect on the tide of humanism?

Yes, God answered their prayer by visiting the American nation. The approximate number of converts during the 40 years of Awakening in America can be determined by examining the membership records of many protestant churches. While some of this increase was through other means, a gain of almost three million within 50 years must be due in part to intensive evangelism.

Today, America stands as one of the most powerful and wealthiest countries in the world. No ordinary human or political effort could have accomplished such a change. Only the miraculous intervention of God who has the power to change not only hearts but also nations, could have orchestrated such a wonderful transformation of America.

ETCHE IN GOD'S AGENDA
Etche people have an appreciable history of participation in the Christian faith. According to history, modern religion penetrated into Etche around 1860. At present, there are over 50 modern religious groups competing for membership in Etche land. We have equally witnessed a

greater number of Etche people attending churches today than before.

Take a drive around various villages and communities in Etche on Sundays, and you will notice men and women going to fellowship in their various denominations. However, the question that demands an urgent answer is: have we had a fair share of God's intervention as a people? Can we truly say that we are enjoying freedom in its true sense? Can we say that Etche is developed by the standard of God? Why are so many people going to churches on Sundays, yet their lives are still the same, without change, and impact? Why have we not occupied some political positions in Rivers State and Nigeria?

These and many more are the questions we will be exploring in the subsequent pages of this section. We will make comparison between Etche and other nations that have received help from God in their quest for development.

it is important to note that Etche ethic nationality is in God' agenda. God has us in mind from the origin of this world. He has destined us for greatness and not stagnation. We are a blessed people and not cursed in any way. An Etche man has the potential to become the Governor of Rivers State, Minister, and Senator of the Federal Republic of Nigeria, even the President and in-Chief of the Federal Republic of Nigeria. We can be all of these by the grace of God?

There are no people that own the birthright to always produce leaders. Leadership is the birthright of all including Etche people. What then is the problem?
It is God that enthrones leaders and exalts a people. Power belongs to God. The scripture says in Psalm 62:11 *"God hath spoken once; twice have I heard this; that power belongeth unto God"*. It is to whomsoever that God desire that he gives power.

What qualifies individuals or nations to obtain God's favour for the gift of power? God has a standard for exalting a nation. Etche people are included in this standard. The secret is captured in Acts 10:34, 35. It reads;

"Then Peter opened his mouth, and said, "of truth I perceive that God is no respecter of persons: But in every nation he that feareth him and worketh righteousness, is accepted by him."

Also in Romans 10:12, 13, God said:

"For there is no difference between the Jew and the Greek: for the same Lord over all is rich unto all that call upon him, for whosoever shall call upon the name of the Lord shall be saved".

These are the underlying secrets behind any societal revolution. These are the easiest and simplest ways to capture the attention of God upon a people. Therefore, I believe that as we get ourselves set to call upon God and seek His righteousness, our exaltation and manifestation are very close.

In the preceding pages, I will be sharing with you the steps and methods required for us to attract the attention of God. The word of God is the first step towards building a sustainable foundation which leads to the topmost top.

CHAPTER FIFTEEN

THE POWER OF GOD'S WORD

———————◆————————◆———————

"No problem is too large for God's intention, and

no person is too small for God's intention

- John Mason

———————◆————————◆———————

What is in the word of God? What is it that makes it unique? Every other book informs, but this book (the Bible) transforms. The word of God is the master key of life. It is able to bring spiritual emancipation and material empowerment to a people. No wonder God said to Joshua in Joshua 1:8; *"This book of the law shall not depart out of thy mouth; but thou shalt mediate therein day and might, that thou mayest observe to do according to all that is written therein: For then, thou shalt make thy way prosperous, and then thou shalt have good success."*

The word of God is at the root of societal development. It is the foundation of reclaiming the Etche dream. It is the tool for re-engineering and rebuilding our communities. The word of God is packaged in the Bible, which I believe is the safest guide for destiny.

The Bible is the most valuable book in the whole world. It is the oldest, yet the most current; the most of all times. It is the most widely quoted of all texts on earth, and its principles still rule the civilized world today. Its laws make up most of the contents of all legal systems worldwide. Its contents touch on all aspects of human existence: spiritual, intellectual, physical, moral, social etc. I believe the Bible is the most dependable and reliable text on leadership principles.

The word of God is light and its light penetrates the invisible with its invincible force and delivers its mission with precision. Its "meat" strengthens the soul and revitalizes the body; Its "light" shatters all darkness and shows the way to go. Its "balm" heals the sick body and sets the afflicted free. Its "sword" destroys all satanic holds and wins all invisible wars. It is "refiner's fire". It sanctifies all lives, and its "principles" edify and establish wisdom.

The word of God controls all the happenings in the world. The written word rules both the natural and spiritual world. Holding fast to the word of God by faith puts one in total command of all activities in this world. Surely, Etche people and the entire world will continue to grope in darkness without the written word of God, including the Etche people.

The realization of Etche agenda will be doomed without the people adhering strictly to the word of God. I am yet to come across a man that regretted his commitment to the practice of the word of God. Many regret ignoring the values contained therein. You are always in command of events by holding fast to the word of God. To toss the Bible aside is to stir up devastating storms in ones life. .

Commitment to the word of God guarantees peace. Adherence to the Bible stimulates transformation which brings joy unspeakable bliss. Truly, this great Book holds the answer to every question and the key to every door.

Every other text is made up of letters, but the Bible is made up of wonders. The effect of every other book is limited to the natural sphere, but the effect of the Book of books transcends the natural to the spiritual and even to eternity. Its effect is supernaturally unlimited; its authority irresistible, and its force unstoppable.

The word of God is for a successful and impactful living. It is a divine visa to a life of exploits, the way out of every trouble. It is the truth about all life issues, and the gateway to a life of fulfillment. The word is designed for profitable living. The more committed Etche people are to its principles, the more profitable life becomes. The word is water, meat, and is able to meet all physical needs. It is the wisdom of God in print, and is able to make wise the simple. The word of God is a spiritual hammer that breaks the rock in pieces. It is the eternal truth about God, man, Etche people, Nigeria, the entire world, and the world that is to come"

The word of God is certainly the principal pillar of destiny. Without it we can do nothing, as all other pillars are built on it. The quality and quantity of the word of God we consume is what determines how great our destiny as a people will be.

Take note that it is not enough to "know" and preach the word; one must practice and 'live" by the word, in order to derive its benefits. Until Etche people allows the word of God to enter their hearts, darkness will continue to reign. If we must shine, then we must have encounter with the word to shine.

Etche People and God's Word
I said earlier that intellectualism, common sense and political calculations will never be enough in our quest to develop our dear Etche. These factors no doubt are very crucial. The word of God is what determines our ultimate worth and repositions us for victory. The revelation of the word of God will reposition Etche people to their rightful places as stakeholders and right citizens of this country, Nigeria.

God's word carries God's life and nature. The scripture says in 2 Peter 1:4: *"whereby are given unto us exceeding*

great and precious promises, that by these ye might be
partakers of the divine nature....

Every scripture is 'pregnant' with divine nature. The more
scriptures you imbibe, therefore, the more of His divine
nature you possess. The word of God inoculates us with
the nature of God, His abilities and capabilities,
connecting us to His divinity. That is what makes the
difference between the Bible and your history, chemistry
or psychology books. Whereas these are all made up of
mere letters and are designed to only inform you, the Bible
is made of wonders; is packaged to transform you and to
change your level and position.

When the word of God permeates your life it begins the
process of transforming your humanity into divinity by
upgrading and translating you. Something changes when
God's word comes or enters into you. That is why Jesus
said: "The words I have spoken to you, they are spirit; they
communicate my power, and they are life; they
communicate my nature". (paraphrase mine)

God has no way of ending our toiling other than through
the knowledge of His word and prayer. We cannot be in
command until the word of God is at hand. When the word
is entrenched in our life, it results in being in charge of the
affairs of life. Most Etche people don't have ideas that are
adequate to handle life challenges they are confronted
with. When knowledge and information in certain areas

become adequate, every door in those areas open on their own. No matter how many devils seem to be challenging us, light is enough to deal with them, as the entrance of God's word gives light and understanding to our simple minds. Knowledge will open any door to which it is directed. The word of God Says: *"And to the angel of the church in Philadephia write: These things saith he that hath the key of David, he that openenth and no man shuffeth and shutteth, and no man openeth."- Revelation 3:7*

Jesus is the one that has the key mentioned above, and who is Jesus? He is the word of God. The word of God delivers to us the key of David, and when he opens, no man shuts, and when He shuts, no man can open. The devil does not have the final say about the doors of our life.

We must all come to the word of life to take delivery of our keys. The Bible is a book of keys and the covenant keys it contains are what we refer to as revelation knowledge, divine insights and illumination.

We need to ask God to help us locate from His word the appropriate keys that deal with the issue before us. The struggles we encounter is because we don't have the appropriate key. How much prayer do you need to pray before you enter into your car without your keys in your hand? In like manner, every door can be opened; all that is needed is the use of the appropriate covenant key. The position and offices we desire can be accessed through the power of God's word.

For the word to gain access into you, you must first pay attention to it. If we don't pay attention to the word of God, we may never take delivery of the keys that operate the issues of life. I have always said that our triumphs and success in life is not a matter of luck, but divine. We need to pay the price to get it! Stay in the control room of the word of God to get what it takes to actually be in control. Remember, every extra light you get puts more of God in you, because God is light and in Him is no darkness at all.

The word of God is the only infallible, invincible instrument of control. It not only puts us in control, it also makes us masters of circumstances and situations.

WISDOM FOR REBUILDING ETCHE

If we make it our first goal to place God first, it solves many problems at once. Education alone is not enough tool for rebuilding Etcheland. We need something more superior to it. This is because education produces more of intellectuals and not necessarily intelligent or wise people.

In my opinion, intelligent people are far superior to intellectuals. Let me briefly explain the difference between intelligence and intellectualism in this context. Intellectuals are products of academics. They receive their knowledge through regulated learning and principles propounded by their teachers. The information that they receive in class are not necessarily new; they are generalized knowledge. Intellectuals take pride in the degree that they parade. For example, a professor may be classified as an intellectual because of the various papers and degrees he parades, but he may not be classified as being intelligent or a man of wisdom. Why, you may ask?

Intelligent people are men of wisdom, insight, foresight and hindsight. The source of their knowledge has been described in many forms. While some assume that the source of their wisdom is from superior beings or unknown gods, others assume that they learn from nature. But the truth is that the source of their knowledge and, inspiration is from God. God is the sole custodian of wisdom, which makes men intelligent.

Intelligent people or men of wisdom operate by vision and revelation. They are originators, creators and pioneers. They don't use others' theories like intellectuals; they propound their own theories. Their pride is not based on their certificates and degrees. Their pride is based on the product and theories they are able to create. Men of wisdom are solution bearers. They are taught and inspired by God himself.

Therefore, the educated class in Etche needs to graduate from being intellectuals to becoming intelligent people, on the senses. It's basically all about intellectual wisdom and stops at academic knowledge. It includes all technological, scientific and intellectual efforts (1 Cor 2:6).

Devilish or diabolical wisdom operates in the occult realm. It is the wisdom of the princes of this world; that is satanic wisdom. It involves the manipulation of the mind through satanic influences.

Divine wisdom, on the other hand, is the wisdom that is from above; God's wisdom. Paul the apostle, by the inspiration of the Holy Spirit, said that all the wisdom of this world and devilish wisdom equal zero when compared with the inexhaustible virtues of the wisdom of God. This wisdom is available to all and sundry via salvation, unlike in occultic circles where there are various degrees of knowledge per time, and the things that are done, are largely shrouded in mysteries. Divine wisdom can be defined as knowing what to do and doing it in order to get the desired result. It is knowing which way to go. Divine wisdom is knowing the scriptural way to go, the scriptural steps to take and the scriptural things to do. It doesn't wait for solutions, but creates solutions to problems with proofs.

Wisdom is not just a product of reasoning; rather, God's wisdom is released by reasoning with Him in the light of men of wisdom. They need to look beyond their certificates and degrees and begin to think of creating original products, theories and practical solutions to the numerous challenges we are facing as a people.

Graduating to this level can only be possible when we encounter the wisdom of God. In the following lines, I will be sharing with you how to encounter the wisdom of God.

WHAT IS WISDOM?

We hear a lot of talk about wisdom both in the world and from scriptures. The American Heritage Dictionary defined it as: "understanding of what is true, right, or lasting; insight, common sense; good judgment; the sum of scholarly learning through the ages; knowledge; wise teaching of the ancient sages; a wise outlook, plan, or course of action".

The Bible describes different kinds of Wisdom. In James 3:15, 17; *"This wisdom descendeth not from above, but is earthly, sensual, and devilish. But the wisdom that is from above is first pure, then peaceable, gentle, and easy to be entreated, full of mercy and good fruits, without partiality, and without hypocrisy".*

There is the earthly wisdom, the sensual, devilish and divine wisdom (wisdom from above). Earthly wisdom is the wisdom of this world, common sense or natural wisdom. Sensual wisdom is men's wisdom; and it centers is the applied knowledge of the truths gleaned from the word of God. This is how Jesus defined wisdom:

"Therefore whosoever heareth these sayings of mine, and doeth them, I will liken him unto a wise men, which built his house upon a rock."- Matthew 7:2

Wisdom is not common sense, but scriptural sense. It is not mere mental exertion or restricted to knowledge alone; but doing the laws of God. It is making use of the word of God to produce profits in any given area of life. That is, doing things God's style, His approach, and by His method. This is a better way of getting results and answers, because God's way and thoughts are higher and better than man's (Isa.55:8-9).

THE SOURCE OF DIVINE WISDOM
Just as everyman's wisdom is expressed in his words; God's word is equally an expression of His wisdom. God's word is the source of divine wisdom. It is His wisdom bank. In His words are hidden all the treasures of wisdom and knowledge (Psa 101:2-3). Wisdom for enjoying a successful family life, buoyant business, societal development and academic excellence are all available in the word.

The knowledge of the truth comes by an encounter with God and His son, Jesus Christ. The correct application of this knowledge is called wisdom. The instructions contained in the Bible are clear and detailed informations that deal with all human affairs. Whatever is declared in it is superior to any circumstance on earth.

No wonder the Psalmist said: *"thou through thy commandments has made me wiser than mine enemies: for they are ever with me." Psalm 119:98*

The Bible makes one wise thus Paul said to Timothy: *"And that from a Child thou hast known the Holy Scriptures, which are able to make thee wise unto salvation through faith which is in Christ Jesus." (2 Timothy 3:15)*

The Bible is God's wisdom packaged in the book form. It is the original wisdom bank that covers all areas of life. This wisdom is the key to exploit excellence, and guarantees rest. Hearing God's word and doing it makes you a wise man.

By the wisdom of God, you are able to control the affairs on this world including life, death and things present and in the future. You are able to regulate and monitor your future.

Here are a few things the Bible says about wisdom:

"I wisdom dwell with prudence, and find out knowledge of witting inventions" (Prouerbs 8:12)
"How much better is it to get wisdom than gold? And to get understanding rather than silver!" (Proverbs 19:8)

"He that getteth wisdom loveth his own soul: he that keepeth understanding shall find good"(Proverbs 19:8)

"Buy the truth, and sell it not; also wisdom and instruction and understanding "(Proverbs 23:23)

Through wisdom is an house built; and by understanding it is established. And by knowledge shall the chambers be filled with all precious and pleasant riches" (Proverbs 24:3-5)

"Who is as the wise man? And who knoweth the interpretation of a thing a man's 'wisdom maketh his face to shine, and the boldness of wisdom, his face shall be changed" (Ecclesiastes 8:1)

"Wisdom is better than strength; wisdom is better than weapon of war" (Ecclesiastes 9:16, 18)

The wisdom of God is our sure guide in our effort to rebuilding, reclaiming and projecting The Next Etche Development Project (NEDEP).

SECTION SIX

DEMANDS OF THE FUTURE

*The crowning fortune of a man is to
be born to some pursuits which find him
employment and happiness, whether it is to
make baskets or broad words
or canals or statues or songs*

-Ralph Waldo Emerson

CHAPTER SIXTEEN

RACE OF MINORITIES

"With each new day in Africa, a gazelle wakes up knowing he must outrun the fastest lion or perish. At the same time, a lion stirs and stretches, knowing he must outrun the fastest gazelle or starve"

- Anonymous

In 2011, I said that the road to pioneering success was still open to serious, dedicated people working for progress. During the following four years, we have added nothing to our previous achievements in Etche, rather, we have only destroyed and continued to destroy our motherland. Nevertheless, I am still convinced that we can overcome and move forward in spite of the challenges.

Whenever we talk about the future, we should be talking in terms of challenges that lie ahead. Our ambitions are big and we anticipate even bigger challenges. Our ability to overcome these challenges depends on our capability to plan, work and feel optimistic and confident about ourselves, our potential and our capacity to reach our goals. Great challenges make great people and when I look back to the past and then to the future, I am convinced we will overcome these challenges and succeed. We did so in the past and can certainly do so again.

For more than 30 years, the ability to overcome challenges and quickly accommodate all sorts of changes has been one of the most important strengths of the Etches. We must adapt quickly to the various and rapid changes ahead. We encounter new challenges and should therefore move comprehensively. It is crucial for us to improve our capability in developing and upgrading education, human resources, social participation, engagement and political representation while expanding our role in the private sector.

We must also streamline our role in the public sector by promoting transparency at all levels and in all industries, expanding investment incentives to reach beyond our territories. We must engage to incubating small and medium enterprises as we upgrade financial programmes for new projects; fight disunity; simplify procedures; and introduce excellence as a basic requirement in all our activities.

Strategically organizing human resources, fostering a better investment environment, upgrading infrastructure, reforming the political structure, strengthening the partnership between the public and private workers, polling public opinion and showcasing for excellence and creativity are basic, prerequisites. We must continually study the best ways to improve and reach innovative solutions that promote efficiency and enhance benefits.

Our society is prone to many negative influences that we do not always pay attention to, even though they have substantial impact on the individual, corporate and social levels. We must rid ourselves of these aspects as quickly as possible by encouraging positive behaviour, promoting honesty and upgrading performance. In the long run, this will lead to positive results. It will enable us to optimize our resources and contribute towards providing an environment that promotes excellence and creativity.

Overcoming the challenges of a new century in a new millennium calls for fresh methodologies and innovative approaches. This, in turn, calls for change. Change also indicates a change of mindset; the ability to understand the language of the today's Nigeria and convey our message, standpoint and goals, in a clear, simple and frank manner. If we achieve this, our neighbours will understand us and allow us to promote better cooperation between them, eliminating sources of misunderstanding and focusing all our efforts on development.

Our goals should be strategic, as are our plans and aspirations, so that the change we are talking about should respond to all of these and match them. During the last 16 years of the return of democracy in Nigeria, I believe we have acquired vast experience in finding innovative political solutions to resolving the problems that will elevate Etche into the modern age. We must, however, be prepared to face the most sensitive and complicated challenges that still lie ahead. This calls for all of us to shoulder our responsibilities, be realistic in our analysis and decisions, distinguish between facts and illusions, and set our goals and priorities precisely, in order to mobilize the resources needed to implement them. If necessary, we must equip ourselves with a strong will to overcome the impossible and walk the extra mile to recognize reconciliation of opposites at any time and on all levels. If anybody thinks we are hopeful of a miracle, I would like to agree with them that challenges often trigger miracles.

On Matters of Peace
When we talk about the future we will be talking about peace. Our people are involved in communal and political conflicts which cause tension, and a breach of peace and stability. These negative aspects nevertheless still hinder us in one way or another. It is therefore evident that there is not enough resolve to secure peace and build stability.

I believe that our politicians are directly responsible for the sorry state of affairs in Etche, because they are the only people, vested with the necessary tools for implementing the resolutions of government. Thus they are the ones capable of leading the Etches towards just and comprehensive solutions.

Achieving sound development and political reform while establishing social justice will cure another aspect of the problem. I believe the effort against cultism should move simultaneously on two fronts: direct security interface and efficient treatment of the causes, which I earlier presented.

While I consider the politicians to be directly responsible for the present situation in the Etche, I am not exonerating the traditional rulers and concerned elders from their responsibilities. Through their actions and inactions, some of us give others excuses or alibis, and do not correctly read the facts of the present system, while others continue to let their sentiments control their decisions.

Avoiding such pitfalls lies in applying reason, justice and logic; focusing on the broader picture instead of getting bogged down by detail. We should concentrate on the survival of Etche rather than its destruction. We must reject crisis outright and give precedence to the interests of people over those of individuals. We do not know of anything in particular we have gained from all the crises Etches have experienced over the past years, but we know that crises have messed us up, delayed the implementation of our projects and postponed development for years.

Some people still believe they can achieve peace through confrontation. These people do not read history correctly. There is no such thing as permanent victory or defeat in the history of mankind. World War I ended with a great victory, but World War II was fiercer and deadlier than all the wars the world had previously witnessed. After several violent communal crises, Etche does not look any closer to peace today than it did twenty years ago. We learn from this that the one who makes peace is more important than the one who wages war.

Democracy
Democracy for us signifies the right to choose. Our fathers never imposed their opinions on us, but rather lead us to the democratic principle of freedom of choice. I am convinced that this is the right way to deal with people, because persuasion is more effective and sustainable than all other methods of enforcement.

Freedom of choice is one of the basic rules of democracy. If democracy was imposed by decree, it will end by decree. If we forced society to adopt a concept such as democracy before allowing it to debate the very concept on the largest scale possible, we would be pushing society into free fall. If we want to impose democracy on people, we would be breaking the most important principles of democracy. It is obvious then, that democracy should not be used as a weapon to threaten, interfere or segregate the people.

Democracy should not be threatening to us, because we have been practicing our own brand of democracy for a very long time. What is possibly frightening are the social, economic and political consequences that could arise if a people's leadership shelves or ignores the real problems that exist, and opts for a dictatorial-style.

If properly practiced, democracy has many benefits and advantages. However it is not a magic portion to cure all kinds of social, economic and political ailments. It does not generate jobs, protect us from recession, guarantee the election of the best candidates, nor prevent crisis or absolutism. Some regimes act as if democracy is a mere process of polling voters, while others, in the name of democracy, violate conventional laws and perpetuate atrocities. There are also those who conveniently forget their electoral promises.

I am not against a democracy that is chosen by the people based on proper evaluation and true conviction. I am also not against any system that maintains security, stability, rights and moral values; or a system that allows freedom of expression, freedom and the right of exercising humanism, rights, customs and traditions.

Skills

Mankind, with machines and capital investment, can conquer the impossible. God blessed us with the knowledge of this fact, enabling us to scan the future and exploit the creative powers of our society. I am convinced that teaching our children properly will perpetuate a new kind of literacy that will equip us in joining the national race.

Success in this race calls for educating new generations - who believe in God, who realize their commitment to their nations - in all kinds of modern disciplines, to qualify them to compete nationally in various fields of modern science. We can only achieve this by upgrading our education qualifications, equipping our people with the latest technological tools, using modern technologies in education. We will join a dynamic academic environment that promotes scientific research, innovation and creativity. This will involve practical and all-inclusive strategy that prioritizes education as a vital pillar of our comprehensive development plan.

Thus when we are forecasting our future, we will be speaking about people with adequate educational qualifications, competencies, potential and independent ways of thinking. We will be developing sustainable local expertise to build up a steady supply of human capital, capable of dealing efficiently with the challenges that lie ahead and providing us the highest levels of quality in productivity.

We must supplement our elementary education with capable institutions that enrich knowledge, promote creativity, encourage innovation and initiatives, motivate ambitions and prepare managerial talents to lead societal businesses.

The prime objective of our present and future development initiatives focuses initially on the social dimension, and consists of introducing comprehensive plans to enrich our human capital and enable our people through education, training and support.

Preparing for the future involves, first of all, training our youths to lead the development process, driven by a sense of their absolute duty to maintain our economic and political evolution. This will encourage them to place their dynamic potential at the service of our society. We have a wealth of young talents, and it is the responsibility of each and every sector of society to nurture them. This can only be done through proper education, training, support and encouragement; and by scouting for special skills and talents, while also nurturing creative initiatives.

Success in development requires excellence in managing our human capital. We expect our youths to excel in trade, industry, management and all other economic activities.

Meanwhile, we will continue to attract skilled and talented professionals who specialize in critical disciplines related to the new knowledge-based economy.

CHAPTER SEVENTEEN

NEXT ETCHE
DEVELOPMENT PROJECT
(NEDEP 2025)

Vision should stir the resolve, creativity and initiative in people and revive their determination to compete

-David Oguzierem

The goal of any visionary leader is to serve his people effectively. Relying on a limited group of people to outline and develop the details of such a vision will result in the kind of visions people do not need. For a vision to meet the interests of people, the leader must know what the people want because they will be the prime beneficiaries of that vision.

Leaders must therefore undertake field surveys in the villages and streets of Etche, in markets, shops and farm settlements, and expand the scope of the dialogue and consultation to the point where it covers the largest possible number of Etche people from every walk of life, including farming, trading, manufacturing, services, management, civil service, politics, education or anything else.

In the next stage, the leader must consult senior citizens and a select group of experts and specialists from the most prominent and dedicated universities, research centres, companies and organizations. The consulting body should cover all aspects related to the vision, including the economic, social and political planning from all around Nigeria. We should then provide them with the outline of the vision and allow them to freely discuss and provide suggestions. Accordingly, the leader may reconsider his vision and amend it if necessary, before revealing its details to the public and converting its elements into a plan

Consulting and conducting surveys are essential tools for planning consensus. Once consensus is achieved, the vision becomes applicable. We must walk this extra mile to give our development plans the human depth it deserves, as well as the necessary state and national dimensions most suited to acquire support for our development aspirations.

We need to study and understand the new concepts and rapid changes taking place around us, before drawing a clear work plan that will accommodate all these factors and help us attain the best results. This will also help us benefit from the experience of others in developing our own capabilities in modern and social sciences and philosophy, thus promoting our competitive powers and securing the right conditions for success and prosperity.

People are the asset of any vision - they make it real. People will not allow the vision to materialize unless they are to convinced about its validity and ascertain if it will meet their expectations and interests while remaining that practical, clear and simple. Everyone must believe that his opinion counts, and that he or she must contribute to the vision. This will generate a sense of ownership.

NEXT ETCHE DEVELOPMENT PROJECT 2025

In projecting the Next Etche Development Project (NEDEP 2025), we must embark on new strategic commercial projects in each of the six clans of Etche nation. The projects will be started and concluded on or before the end of the year 2025. The projects are listed below. This is the background for our vision for Etche until 2025.

It is a systematic, ambitious and comprehensive economic and political vision, essentially focused on people and wealth creation. We believe that we have the power, resources and determination to realize it the way we want. We can summarize the objectives of the vision as follows:

1. Promoting our state and national competitive powers by:
a. Demanding and lobbying for Etche State.
a. Lobbying and securing additional four Local Government Areas for Etche people.
b. Identifying with all viable political parties in Nigeria.
c. Supporting our sons and daughters to contest and win the Senate and governorship position in Rivers State.
d. Lobbying and securing appointment into state and

2. Implementing a number of new strategic projects on schedule in each of the six clans of Etche nation.
     I. Igbo Agwuru-Asa : Etche Industrial City
     ii. Ozuzu Clan: Etche University
     iii. Omuma Clan: Etche Specialist Hospital
     iv. Mba Clan: Etche International Farm Estate
     v. Okehi Clan: Etche International Market
     vi. Ulakwo/Umuselem : Etche Sports Stadium

3. Increasing the graduates of Etche heritage by 100 percent.
4. Connecting all parts of Etche to national electricity grid.
5. Constructing and completing all roads in Etche.
6. Increasing economic activities in Etche by 100 %.
7. Allocating a crucial role to youths in implementing the vision, through focused initiatives that will enrich our human resources and contribute to supporting entrepreneurship, and qualify our people to shoulder their responsibilities in the development process.
8. A commitment to keep pace with social and economic development, in order to attain an ideal social balance.
9. Promote the role of women, assert social values and promote   tolerance.

Although some of these goals are quite ambitious, I am well aware of our strengths and weaknesses, and I am not proposing anything that is beyond our capabilities.

I have previously said that it is about time the Etche dream had a chance to awaken and become a vision of reality. I years of regression and marginalization are but a blink of an eye in history. This may sound optimistic, it is an optimism based on facts and not illusion. We have all we need to engage in a great development process, both now and the future

The pillars are strong but lying low, the doors are large but they are not open, the walls are high but separated from each other. We therefore need to find leaders capable of raising those pillars to the sky, opening the doors to the world and breaking down walls that prevent Etches from meeting one other and participating in development. Can we do it? I am sure we can, but we first have to regain the pioneering spirit we have lost in leadership and in society.

The Etche leader must be loyal to his people and committed to realizing their dreams and ambitions based on a clear and modern vision. In social terms, we have to get rid of all obsolete aspects of our life and engage in dialogue with other ethnic nationalities. It is equally important for us to remove all kinds of misunderstanding and promote cooperation and friendship with other ethnic nations, we will win in politics, manufacturing, technology, trade, education, culture and all other related fields.

Let us forget all the ado surrounding us, ignore threats, discussions about our heritage, tension and hollow words about conflicts between us. Seeking the approval of others is one thing and seeking the interest of Etche is another. Our tendency to lose great opportunities in the past can be treated and compensated by availing ourselves of the present ones and providing the right conditions for making even greater ones. The policy we have to adopt is to prepare ourselves for the great political and economic race - and then go on to win it.

.Marching forward

Achieving success requires taking the right decision at the right moment. Such decisions were at the very foundation of Etche's success during the era of the Nwukes, Anuchas, and Opurum, and we are confident that the decisions we are taking now will make Etche even more successful in the future. Each one of us has the right to dream and to have our own visions, goals and time frames to achieve them. All leaders dream, but only a true leader can turn a dream into a vision and a reality.

Vision is the way to true development and is also a matter of courage and conquering the impossible. It is believing in our ability to achieve our goals; having clear objectives and realizing them with determination, efficiency and speed, never pausing until our children see their ethnic nationality competing with the others.

I believe that I have provided sufficient evidence in this book to say that achieving success is a realistic goal, not only for you, but for the whole of the Etches. I also believe that upgrading the political and economic role of the Etches from local to national level is a natural development. In order to keep the momentum going, we must focus on developing a knowledge-based economy and human resources to reach the high economic growth rate we aspire to.

We do not want to find ourselves, anytime in the future, pawns to a single source of income, and will always observe the need to diversify and avail ourselves of all suitable opportunities. We should not be content to catch up with others, but we should aspire to be successful and to show pioneering role.

We want that pioneering status in full and will not settle for anything less. We want it not only for your own sake, but for the sake of all Etches. Catching up with others comes at a price, but attaining a pioneering role has an even greater price. Our forefathers taught us that great harvest is not gotten at the backyard, rather it is gotten in the deep forest. We must therefore be prepared for anything and everything, no matter how hard this might be.

Every ethnic nation wants to be a winner and each one is prepared for the great race - one that is likely to become the greatest race this country has ever known. I have often been asked where the challenges going on in Etche today will lead us and my only answer is: "To victory."

This, however, is not the only answer. There are others related to the education we have enjoyed, our motives in life and what we want to achieve. If my motive is the progress of my people to the status they deserve, at what point should I stop? What progress would we have achieved if we had all stopped?

If anyone bragged about the goals they have achieved, chances are that they will not be able to achieve any more. When we are at the beginning of the road there is no time for bragging. What lies ahead of us is much, much more than we have done to date.

Because the horizon has no limits, a vision cannot have any boundaries. The closer you come to the horizon, the more the boundaries extend. A visionary leader must match these new boundaries with new aspirations in order for his people to provide magnificent opportunities for the society. We will keep pushing our vision forward. Those who succeed us, their successors and all those thereafter until the end of time, will forge ahead along the same road.

If time went in a full circle, we would have accomplished what we have achieved during the past 20 years in just eight years. But since acquiring skills, knowledge and experience never stops, we will double what we have achieved during the past 20 years in the coming eight years. If this does not give you an idea about what we have in store for the future, then let me summarize it one final time.

Life consists of a number of opportunities and great opportunities do not come knocking on people's doors. Whoever wants such opportunities must grab them when they arise, for his people and for himself. We have to be powerful, strong-willed, determined and willing to grasp such opportunities, so that we do not have to scavenge for the leftovers.

I will never abandon one opportunity and wait for another. We have not reached the goal we are striving for. What you see now is nothing compared to our vision... just tiny parts of what lies ahead.

We will build a great monument on these foundations and it is my wish that every Etche person will follow suit so that we can develop Etche nation into a people of excellence. The hand of the Etches is reaching out to join the hands of its Niger Delta brothers; so take it and let us start building together.

I know the road to development and modernization is difficult; and long I also know that the next stages will be even tougher and longer. But I have faith in God; I believe in my people, in the wisdom of our emerging leadership and the future of our Next Etche. I am confident we will realize our goals. Our vision is clear, our road is paved and the clock is ticking. There is no more time for hesitation or half-baked goals or solutions. Development is an ongoing process and the race for success has no finishing line. Lets begin the now as to realize all our goals by 2025.

CHAPTER EIGHTEEN

NO EASY VICTORIES

In the confrontation between the stream and the rock, the stream always wins, not through strength but by perseverance.

H. Jackson Brown

I believe it is high time we came out of our deplorable state, and positively change our identity by first improving our lot as individuals. It is a changed people that result in a changed land. That is getting to know what to do, going ahead to do it, and thereby moving ahead. It is time to take our destinies in our hands, and make the most of it.

In my opinion, when you give people a purpose, they will be committed, get them committed, and they will be creative, then productive, and successful. That is the purpose of this book.

We can make our lives sublime and worthy. All we need is to acquire the requisite information and intelligence with a sense of mission. This will result in outstanding change and impact in Etche land. Zig Ziglar said, *"Just any dummy can succeed, if he cares to know what it takes"* There cannot be a move without a mover. This book is all about the projection of our future empowerment agenda and the reengineering of our socio-political system as Etche people. It will change our approach, so as to bring about the socio-economic transformation we have long desired.

In the words of Dr. Martin Luther King Jr, *"Change does not roll in on inevitability, but comes through continuous struggle. And so we must straighten our backs and work for our freedom. A man can't ride you unless your back is bent."* He also said **"Freedom is never voluntarily given by the oppressor; it must be demanded by the oppressed.**

Our destiny is in our hands. Life is a struggle. We are the architect of our future. We are 100% responsible for our empowerment as a people. Nobody will empower us. We **MUST** struggle for our freedom and empowerment.

Our time of empowerment and liberation is NOW. Let us rise for the struggle. Victory is ours. This will definitely be our experience.

I therefore challenge you to pay your price for Etche, in order that we may win the prize.

I challenge you to suspend you personal interests for our collective aspiration as a people.

I challenge you to step out with courage and, make sacrifices that will position Etche at top.

I challenge you today to seek to be a better ambassador to Etche nation.

I challenge you to increase your support to our good leaders and withdraw your support from bad leaders.

I challenge you to encourage and support the mass and free education of Etche people.

I challenge you to look out for an Etche son or daughter that is not able to go to school due to poverty and give him/her scholarship today.

I challenge all graduates to seek higher education so that the number of PhD holders and professors in our midst will increase.

I challenge you to become an entrepreneur, professional and expert in any field you have chosen.

I challenge you to be a better Christian. You must understand that the love of God means love for your fellow Etche man.

I challenge you to pursue peace and unity in Etche.

I challenge you to renounce violence and war, in that it does no man any good.

I challenge you to exercise your constitutional rights by voting in good leaders and voting out the bad ones.

I challenge you to live, love and lead Etche nation to greater heights.

I challenge you to sacrifice and invest your abilities, education and ability for the Etche cause. It is a struggle and we must consider it as such.

I challenge you to lead well if you are privileged to be in position of trust. Etche people are not for sale. Therefore you must not betray them in the course of your duty. The right time to act is NOW.

Long live Etche nation.
Cheta ala Etche, mee ya nma

CHAPTER NINETEEN

REFLECTIONS ON POLITICS, LEADERSHIP, MARGINALIZATION, AND APATHY IN ETCHE

By
Engr. Sam O. Nwankwo

POLITICS

P olitics involves the acquisition and use of power to influence decisions that affect people in a particular group, society and country. Politics is synonymous with leadership and encompasses a wide range of activities and issues. It is associated with struggle and control of power, policy and law making, advocacy, debate, elections, political parties etc.

Many people who are involved in politics do not fully understand the concept and practice of politics. They think of politics as being associated with belonging to political parties, voting during elections and thereafter share and occupy positions and control resources.

The principal aim of participating in politics should be to serve the interest of the people, develop the area and create empowerment opportunities through education and equitable distribution of wealth. Therefore politics should be concerned about service, humanity and carrying the people along. People who get involved in politics should be individuals who are naturally inclined to serve the people and fashion out the best way in which the society could move forward. They should be selfless in all their dealings as they bother about the problems of the society.

There is a vacuum created in Etche land presently due to the absence of naturally endowed political leaders. Honesty and service to the people have become history in today's political scene. In the second Republic, politics in Etche was germane, as superior ideas and logic held sway and anyone who was a mediocre never took the front row in the politics of the time. This made the issue of violence nearly absent during campaigns. Today violence is a regular occurrence in politics and criminal activities have caused dislocation of lives and properties in Etche land.

Etche politicians have taken Etche people for granted because Etche people have been complaisant. This implies that both the political leaders and their followers have defaulted in their respective responsibilities, which has resulted in bad governance, deprivation and denial of the dividends of democracy.

The way forward is that political leaders in Etche should refrain from being undemocratic. Political leaders should practice inclusive governance where the opinions and suggestions of all citizens are sought and utilized through genuine representatives. They should render genuine and selfless service to the people.

The followers or the electorate should be courageous and stand for the sanctity of their votes during elections. Every Etche man and woman should be at alert about the processes that would guarantee a free and fair election and usher in credible people that will genuinely transform the lives of our people.

The electoral umpires, INEC and RISEC officials in the region must be transparent and impartial in the discharge of their duties. Electoral bodies should be granted full autonomy that will ensure efficiency and freedom from undue influence by anybody or individual.

Judicial independence must be ensured so that the abuse of judicial processes will be resisted and the will of the people should be protected from abuse or being truncated by the political class.

Good governance resulting from transparent elections and genuine actions of politicians and the polity will guarantee equitable utilization of our resources for award of scholarships to our children, construction of good roads and bridges, provision of portable water, constant electricity, the establishment of industries, small and medium enterprises, building and equipping of schools and vocational centers and health institutions etc. Etche people will thus begin to enjoy the dividends of good democratic governance.

LEADERSHIP

Richard D. Irwin defines leadership as "the ability to influence people so that they will work to achieve the goal of the leader or the group the leader represents". From the above, one can see leadership as a relationship between one individual and a group of people where influence is exercised by one upon a larger number. Essentially leadership attempts to influence others to act or think in certain ways. Therefore, people are said to be leaders when they succeed in influencing others to do something towards achieving a common goal, which serves the interest of both of them. According to William Shakespeare: some are born great, some achieve greatness; others have greatness trusted upon them. Thus leadership exists under three main groups: There is the formal leader who assumes power through some conventional processes or stipulated conditions for ascending to such position. The leader must qualify before he can lead e.g. chiefs, kings etc. Charismatic leaders possess quality, personal character or charisma that inspires others to follow them; they have the natural capacities or qualities which mark them out to lead. They are said to be born leaders.

A functional leader has the leadership role thrust upon him because he has what the group consider necessary for the achievement of group's goal. Such a leader would likely be nominated, appointed, selected or accredited from among equals. Among the groups, leaders exhibit styles which differentiate one from another. In the democratic style of leadership, the leader is group centered. He interacts and discusses with his subordinates and listens to their advice and suggestions before taking decision. The authoritative leader lords it over the followers. Here the leader makes decision and announces to the people and expects implementation without questioning. He gets work done through fear or "eye" service. A leadership style that combines or takes a little from the two described above is known as Pseudo democrat. Here the leader demonstrates democratic ideals to the group whereas in reality he is intentionally autocratic. He merely involves the group in pretence to support his preconceived decision and views.

The above narrative is intended to educate one on leadership principles so that one can understand the type of leaders that have influenced the Etche nation over the years. From the year 1960 when the Nigerian nation attained independence till date, Etche ethnic nationality has produced several notable leaders among who are; Chief Hon. J.H.E Nwuke, Chief Jonah Akor, Chief S.O Achonwa, Chief M.E Nwankwo, Eze E.N.B Opurum, Eze Dr. D.U Anucha, Dr. Eze Nwala, Chief Nwanoru Okere, Eze. O. Nwodim, Chief Barr. S.O. Nwogu, Chief James Nweke, Prof. Nwankwoala, Prince Emma Anyanwu, Barr. Obi Njoku, Captain Sunday Nwankwo, Eze Ken Nwala, Bishop Okechukwu Nwala etc.

Based on their peculiar leadership styles, Eze E.N.B Opurum and Prince Emma Anyanwu are being highlighted.

HIS EMINENCE, EZE ENB OPURUM

Eze Opurum is a forefront statesman who worked fastidiously with Chief Dr. H.J.R Dappa-Biriye and others to actualize the creation of Rivers State. He joined the Niger Delta Congress (NDC) which allied with NPC (Northern People Congress) to fight for the creation of Rivers State. Eze Opurum helped to set up the first administrative office of Rivers State Government in Bonny.

Eze Opurum fought for the integration of Etche into Rivers State. He worked hard and made a lot of sacrifices for Etche emancipation. After the war, he protected Etche people and promoted their economic welfare. Eze Opurum served the Rivers State government as the Commissioner for Rural Development and Social Welfare from 1974. During his tenure as Commissioner, he drew up the proposal for the establishment of Risonpalm Estate in Etche and Ikwerre, planned and built the model schools - GSS Okehi and Ndashi and built many UPE schools in Etche.

The traditional and chieftaincy institutions in Etche were boosted by Eze Opurum's wisdom and knowledge. Thus when the recognition of chiefs in former Eastern Nigeria was approved in Lancaster house, London and delegated to Nigeria for perfection, Etche was separated from Ikwerre/ Etche council and approved for a traditional authority which is called the "Onye-ishi-Etche". Thereafter, Prince Emmanuel Ben Opurun was unanimously elected the Onye-Ish- Etche by the good people of Etche. Till date, His Eminence, Eze E.N.B Opurum, the Ochie of Etche is the holder of the traditional title of the Onye-ishi-Etche. Eze Opurum is a model man and a visionary leader. He is a great man indeed.

PRINCE EMMA ANYANWU

The man Prince Emma Anyanwu belongs to the group of Charismatic leaders. He made his debut into the political turf a long time ago when most of his contemporaries were ignorant of the system. Prince Emma's style of politics is very peculiar because unlike many other political giants he never contested for an elective position and has never enjoyed any political appointment, but he has always been in the center of all political contests in Etche land. In fact in Etche politics, Emma Anyanwu is known as the kingmaker because he ensures the success of any side he supports. He deploys all his resources to ensure victory. He has been a member of the leading political parties in the country where he ensures that Etche people are equitably represented.

Prince Emma Anyanwu plays visible role in other areas of endeavor. In the traditional/chieftaincy affairs, the Prince plays determinant role even though he is not a title holder. Prince Emma Anyanwu is also a philanthropist. He has trained so many indigent Etche students in both secondary and tertiary institutions. Many love him while some others do not understand him. Though most times he holds sway with unchangeable command but his views hold rigid truth.

The problem of Etche in recent times has been attributed to leadership. This leadership deficit is caused by disunity among the leaders. In times past, when Etche nation made reasonable impact in development, their leaders always met to forge a common cause. Today our leaders who are mainly young politicians operate in separate political fiefdoms, where they not only hold sway but from where they launch missiles at each other. Why is it difficult for these leaders: Ogbonna Nwuke, Ephraim Nwuzi, Alwell Onyeso, Emma Anyanwu, Nnamdi Okere, Captain Nwankwo, Ambrose Nwuzi, Golden Chioma, Reginald Ukwuoma, Kelechi Nwogu, Emeka Nwogu, Nwuke Anucha, to come from their respective political parties and meet to discuss the progress of Etche with some Elders including, Eze Opurum, Obi Njoku, Ben Chioma, Isaiah Choko, Machi Nwodim, Hycent Anuonye and many others? Thereafter they can return to their parties to implement decisions reached.

It will therefore be expedient for Etche politicians to form a political umbrella organization such as Etche National Vanguard Group. This group will ensure that all decision reached in the proposed meetings are implemented.

Etche people are blessed with abundant human and material resources waiting to be harnessed and managed by their leaders. The youths are watching how the present crops of leaders are toying with their future. Etche leaders should quickly unite to create a common cause that will make Etche great and by so doing will etch their names in the golden plaques of posterity. They should note that:

> *"Lives of great men all reminds us*
> *That we can make our lives sublime*
> *And departing leave behind us*
> *Foot prints on sands of time"*

There is a silver lining in the horizon regarding the leadership situation in Etche land. A new crop of leaders are emerging. Among them are Eze Ken Nwala, Captain Sunday Nwankwo and Bishop Okechukwu Nwala. They are young, vibrant and enterprising men, who could have been complaisant in the comfort zones of their various businesses. They decided to sacrifice self for the service of their motherland Etche. They will bring their acumen in their various endeavors to lead Etche to the Promised Land. We wish them more grease to their elbows.

To those others who are in limbo in other lands both in this country and in Diaspora, who refuse to participate in the affairs of Etche land, we only wish them a change of heart so that their plight will not follow these lines:

> *"Breathes there the man with soul so dead*
> *Who never within him had said*

This is my own, my native land
Whose heart has never within him burned.
As home his footsteps he has turned
From wandering on a foreign strand
If such there breathes, go mark him well
For him no mistral raptures swell
High though his title power and pelf
The wretch concentrated all in self
And doubly dying shall go down
To the vile dust from whence he sprung
Unwept, unhonoured and unsung"

MARGINALIZATION

People are said to be marginalized when they are isolated and made to feel irrelevant in the scheme of things which results to exploitation and deprivation. This definition is apt enough to describe the plight of Etche People among other ethnic peoples. Honestly, Etche people have been marginalized!

The issue of whether Etche people are marginalized or not has also been a subject of controversy in recent times. Those who feel strongly that Etche people are marginalized, including the President General of Ogbakor Etche and many Etche elites, are very passionate about it to the extent that they are wont to declare it to the entire world through world press conference or other possible medium.

In reacting to the issue of Etche marginalization, the Onye-Ishi Etche, the man whose name was mentioned to buttress the fact that Etche people are not marginalized had this to say "The Igbo nation in which the Etche people were integrated into (within the period) colonized the land and had an overwhelming influence on the people...and rather than seeing the Etche man as part of itself, used the Etche man to satisfy selfish interest. In fact the Eastern Nigerian Government encouraged their kith and kin to advance into the nooks and crannies of Etche land converting nearly all economic activities in the land to their own advantage". All these happened when an Etche man was in the Eastern Regional House serving the nation.

The Onye-Ishi-Etche went further to say that "Etche has contributed to the economic development of the state and the country, but it is regrettable that the kingdom in turn has not been a beneficiary of the largesse that emanates from the state...Etche people did not participate actively in the agitation of minority groups which led to the Wilinks Commission, thus when the Commission's recommendation were published, Etche was not considered."

Similarly, in 2014 when all other nationalities had their delegates invited to the National Conference, Etche ethnic nationality was excluded despite efforts made by Ogbako Etche. Someone can say that Ogonis were invited after they reacted. Yes! Ogonis are used to reacting and being considered. Other numerous nationalities that attended neither shouted nor ruffled feathers to be included. In this 2014 National Conference the ethnic nationalities that attended shared states and local governments among themselves while Etche people were not considered.

In 1990, a group of women and children from Umechem Community in Etche demonstrated peacefully against their being neglected by Shell Company, an oil giant prospecting for oil in the area. Consequently the security agents of government carried out a gruesome massacre of over 200 people in Umechem.

A paramount ruler of the area, HRH, Eze A.A Ordu, was killed with his sons in the incident. Till date no adequate consideration or compensation has been made to assuage the unpleasant situation just because it happened in Etche. Compare this with the Odi incident and the aftermath of it and make your conclusions.

In the federal and the state governments, Etche people have been denied appointments to important positions such as minister, ambassador, speaker, chairmen of boards and parastatals etc. How do other ethnic nationalities "react" to get considered in these positions? Etche people are expected to react physically before they can be considered relevant to these appointments.

Presently, Etche people have been denied the senatorial slot that should rightly be zoned to them. The two major parties have field an Okrika man and an Ikwerre man respectively in the elections for the senate position.

Among the three ethnicities, the Ikwerre, Etche and Okrika that belong to the Rivers East Senatorial District, the Ikwerres and the Okrikas have each occupied the seat twice while Etche has not been there once. Since the two major political parties are not the only parties participating in the elections, Etche people will definitely relate to any other party or parties that field Etche persons for the senatorial seat not minding the reasons and permutations that are being advanced to deny Etche its right.

Let it be said emphatically that Etche people have been marginalized over a long period of time. Any person or persons that say that Etche people are not marginalized are themselves marginalizing Etche people by mincing words to skew opinions.

APATHY

Apathy is a state of being uninterested or not enthusiastic about anything. Many Etche sons and daughters are apathetic in the affairs or circumstances concerning Etche people or Etche ethnic nationality. This unconcerned attitude is manifested in politics, associations, culture, religion and even extended to family matters.

Apathy in politics or lack of political awareness is an inhibiting factor in the development of Etche land. When one is not interested in politics he or she does not know anything about the concept or practice of politics. Thus when those who have adequate experience and knowledge in management of resources exhibit laissez-faire attitude in politics, they inadvertently leave politics for neophytes. When these inexperienced people get into political positions and act within the limits of their knowledge and abilities, their performances fall short of standards and expectations. This results in bad governance, deprivation and marginalization.

Apathy in associations especially the Ogbako Etche by the people of Etche has greatly and adversely affected the organization. Many adult citizens of Etche tend to dismiss the existence of Ogbako Etche. Some of these people do not know the purpose and functions of the association. During one of the public interactive sessions organized by the association, a prominent Etche chief told the audience that he thought that the association is an exclusive club of some selected elites. Many people share the same belief with the Chief as was discovered on that occasion. Those who have little or no knowledge of Ogbako Etche can be excused but those who have actively participated or have had dealings with the Ogbako Etche cannot be excused when they later exhibit apathy towards the association.

This apathetic cankerworm in Etche people has deprived the Ogbako the funding and patronage needed to manage the affairs of the association. Apathy has also resulted in low attendance of the people to annual conventions of Ogbako Etche. When the expected number and caliber of people fail to attend Ogbako congresses, the debate, opinions and decisions that emanate from such audience will be scanty and substandard. The resultant effect is that Etche people will be found lacking in actions and consequently suffer deprivation and marginalization.

Apathy in Etche cultural practice has created the loss of identity and heritage among the people. So many people use religion and exposure to foreign habits to practice negligence of their own culture. They deride those who engage in cultural practices as inferior people. This attitude has resulted in exodus of people during festive periods and the loss of income from tourism and hospitality.

CHAPTER TWENTY

SPECIAL RECOGNITION

*Nothing can stop an idea whose
time has come - Anonymous*

CHIEF ALLWELL ONYESOH

Whenever the final political history of Etche is written, I am very certain that the name of Chief Allwell Onyesoh would merit a prominent passage. Chief Allwell symbolizes perhaps the very best of patriotism in an epoch where Etche politicians are thinking of themselves and their immediate family alone.

Here is one Etche son who has never appeared to want to be anyone else, anything else but Allwell Onyesoh. Chief Allwell has indisputable political sagacity and courage. He has been and still remains one of the finest politicians that Etche can offer and it is most gratifying for me as an Etche son to note the very wide acceptability which his personality commands across Rivers State. He has single handedly raised and mentored so many growing politicians in Etche and across the state.

Chief Allwell has empowered, engaged and employed more people in the history of Etche than any other politician, dead or alive. As the Commissioner for Education in 1999, he employed and promoted so many Etche people as Principals and Vice Principals across the state. As the Chairman of Rivers State Post Primary Schools Board in 2011, he assisted in the employment of hundreds of Etche sons and daughters into the civil service as teachers.

When Chief Allwell Onyesoh is hated or criticized by his political foes, it is usually because of his life political stand. He believes that it is either you are in or out. There is no standing on the fence in the game of politics. No individual is perfect. Allwell is Allwell and can never become David just as David is David and can never become Allwell. Chief Allwell Onyesoh believes that it is not the position that defines a person; rather it is a person that defines the position.

Chief Allwell is locally called "Onye Nme Nme" because of the high political charisma and influence that he commands. He inserted the word 'politics' into my life's dictionary. I consider him a hero and see him as a living legend. He has served Etche and Rivers State at different times and levels.

Chief Allwell has attempted thrice to represent Rivers East Senatorial District at the national assembly. First was in

2003 and secondly in 2007, the then Governor of Rivers State, Dr Peter Odili, pleaded with him to allow Sen. Thomson Sekibo from Okrika to run. The third time Chief Allwell attempted to grab the position was in 2015, he also stepped down following appeal from the APC party hierarchy to allow Chief Andrew Uchendu from Ikwerre extraction to also represent the zone.

It is important to note that having denied the Etches the opportunity to represent the senatorial district at the national assembly all these years, there is a gentle man agreement that the Etches should be allowed to take a shot at the Senate unchallenged in 2019.

In my humble opinion, Chief Allwell Onyesoh is eminently qualified to represent not just Etches, but Rivers East Senatorial District at the National Assembly.

PROFESSOR OZO-MEKURI NDIMELE

Professor Ozo-Mekuri Ndimele was born 13th August, 19 63 to the union of Chief and Mrs. M. A. Nwaugha in Ogida, Etche. He attended St. Joseph's Secondary School, Umuaturu, where he obtained a West African School Certificate (WASC) in 1979. He proceeded to the University of Port Harcourt where he graduated with a

Bachelor of Arts degree in English in 1985, graduating as the best English Language Student. In 1987, he obtained a Master of Arts degree and bagged a Doctorate of Philosophy degree in Comparative Grammar, in 1991, all from the same University.

The erudite scholar began his career as a lecturer with the Rivers State College of Education, Port Harcourt, Nigeria, in 1987. He has had a steady and consistent progress in his profession. He currently lectures in the Department of Linguistics and Communication Studies, Faculty of Humanities, University of Port Harcourt. He has to his credit numerous publications in nationally and internationally recognised journals. He has authored eighteen books, including 'Echie Grammar'

Professor Ndimele who is the National President of two professional bodies: Linguistic Association of Nigeria, and English Language Teachers Association of Nigeria was Chairman, Etche Education/Scholarship Committee; Secretary of the Port Harcourt Branch of the Nigerian Field Society; Ex-governor, Etche Association of Friends, Coordinator, Etche Water and Sanitation Project and former Head of Department of Linguistics & Communication Studies, University of Port Harcourt. He who is currently a member of Rivers State Government Economic Advisory Committee had served as Public Relations Officer of Ogbakor Etche. He is also on the

Board of the Nigerian Educational Research Development Council, as well as a Member of the Rivers State Scholarship Board. He had served in the Rivers State Post Primary Schools Board. He was the former Dean of the Faculty of Humanities, University of Port Harcourt.

CAPTAIN SUNDAY NWANKWO

On the 14th of June 2014, he hosted a press conference with Rivers State based media executives, including my humble self as the publisher of Time Express newspaper. During the meeting, he lamented on issues affecting Rivers State in general and with particular concern to Etche as it regards unemployment, underdevelopment and insecurity.

Captain Nwankwo is an Etche man by blood and heart. We have so many Etche men by blood, not by heart. But Captain Nwankwo is a patriotic Etche man. He passionately loves Etche and its people. In most of his conversations, the destiny and future of Etche people come first. He has single-handedly made so many Etche young millionaires through offshore employment.

Capatain Nwankwo is a great pioneer in the spirit. To every Etche man, it was an impossible task to attempt to contest the no one position in Rivers State but going by his antecedent, I was not surprised but proud of the milestone achievements which broke the jinx of Etche sons and daughters not contesting the governorship of Rivers State. It has been very difficult to see an Etche man that will spend millions of naira in a contest that will champion the general interest of Etche people. This was in furtherance to the hundreds of oil and gas employment opportunities given to Etche sons and daughters which ordinarily he could have converted to his personal financial benefits.

In summary, let me mention but a few of his achievements in many areas politically.

1. He single handedly brought a relatively new political party to Rivers State.
2. He created an opportunity for an Etche son to become a state party chairman for the first time in history.
3. He single-handedly set up and fund a party structure in the twenty-three local governments of Rivers State.
4. He also purchased Peoples Democratic Party gubernatorial form for 2015 general election.
5. He was screened and given approval by the PDP 2015 gubernatorial primaries screening committee to contest the primaries alongside four other candidates; Senator Lee Maeba, Hon. Michael West and Barr. Nyesom Ezenwo Wike, who became the eventual winner. Over 26 candidates picked the intent form for the primaries.

7. He showcased capacity and was invited by the then President and Commander-in-Chief of the Federal Republic of Nigeria, His Excellency, Dr Goodluck Ebele Jonathan for a meeting considering his political ambition and interest.

8. He was appointed as a member of PDP Presidential Campaign Committee, alongside Dr. Jerry Gana, Dr. Ifeanyi Uba, Chief Turner and a few other eminent Nigerians.

9. Considering Captain Nwankwo Campaign Organization's capacity, his Director-General, Barr. Obi Njoku had the priviledge to be invited for a meeting with President Goodluck Jonathan at the Presidential Villa.

This record breaking achievement has become a political standard that we must continually seek and pursue with vigor in the years to come.

DR. IKECHI G. A. NWOGU

Dr. Godpower Anyalebechi Ikechi Nwogu is a great pioneer in the spirit. He has constantly pushed back the of frontiers of injustice, ignorance and poverty. Dr Nwogu began his teaching career in 1974 with County Grammar School, Ikwerre/Etche. He served as the Principal of Etche Girls Secondary School Umuola-Etche between 1977-1978. In later part of 1978, he was transferred as the Principal of Government Secondary School, Egbolom Abua and he was there until 1979. He joined the service of College of Arts and Science in 1982 and was appointed the Head of Mathematics Department, College of Arts and Science between 1984-1985. He later served as the Head of Technical Sciences Department, between 1986-1988. He also served the institution as the Director of Mathematics Centre between 1989-1991. Dr Nwogu was also appointed Co-ordinator of Matriculation Examination Programme (MEP) in RIVCAS, Port Harcourt between 1992-1994. He later became the Head of Technical Sciences Department, (RIVCAS) between 1994-1996.

In recognition of his outstanding scholarly contributions, extra-curricular ingenuity and leadership artistry, in the year 2000 he was appointed the Acting Provost, College of Arts and Science, Port Harcourt. Two years later, he was confirmed the Provost, Rivers State College of Arts and Science, Rumuola, Port Harcourt. At his exit from the service of RIVCAS, he was again recognized and appointed the Director, Port Harcourt Study Centre, National Open University of Nigeria (NOUN) between

2010-2014. In recognition of his years of uninterrupted dedication to service and a life of unparalleled integrity, the Executive Governor of Rivers State, Barr. Nyesom Ezenwo Wike appointed him as a Commissioner in Rivers State Civil Service Commission in 2015.

Dr Nwogu is a member of relevant professional bodies and academic institutions locally and internationally where he continued to play active roles. He is a member of Philosophy of Education Association of Nigeria. Member, Mathematics Association of Nigeria; Member, Mathematics Society of Nigeria; Fellow, Institute of Corporate Administration of Nigeria (FCIA); Fellow, Institute of Corporate Resource Management (FCRMI); Fellow, Institute of Administrative Management of Nigeria (FIAMN).

DR. GEORGE CHIMEZIE NWAEKE

Dr. George Chimezie Nwaeke was born on 17 November, 1963 in Umukamanu Omuma to Mr. Augustine Iwejor Nwaeke and Mrs. Eunice Nwefere Nwaeke (nee Nwele).
He attended State School Umuogba, Ornuma, between 1971-1976, where he obtained a First School Leaving Certificate. Between 1976-1981, he attended the prestigious County Grammar School, Ikwere/Etche, obtaining a West African School Certificate/General

Certificate on Education. He proceeded to the Rivers State University of Science and Technology, Nkpolu, Port Har court, graduating with a Bachelor of Science (Hons) degree (Accounting), in 1987. In 1993, he obtained Master of Business Administration (MBA), from the same University.

The high point of his profession was his obtaining the ACA of Institute of Chartered Accountant of Nigeria (ICAN) in 1993.

Mr. Nwaeke had served in both private and public sectors, as a teacher between 1981 and 1983; Accounting Lecturer at University of Cross River State (now University of Uyo), between 1987 and 1988. Audit Team Leader, Okuruens and Co. Chartered Accountants; Lecturer, Rivers State University of Science and Technology, Port Harcourt, between December, 1988 and July, 1995. He transferred his services to the Ministry of Finance and Economic Planning as Chief Accountant and then posted to Ministry of Agriculture and Natural Resources, in August 1997, as Director, Finance and supplies.

In 1997, he was appointed Chairman, Audit Panel into the Affairs of Risonpalm. He also holds the position of the Financial Secretary, Port Harcourt District Institute of Chartered Accountants of Nigeria (ICAN) between June, 1997 and September, 1998. Financial Secretary,

Ornuma Progressive Movement (OPM). He is at present the President, Omuma Friends Forum (OFF).

Between July, 1998 and May, 1999, he served as Chairman, Care-taker Committee, Abua/Odual Local Government Area of Rivers State. He was the former Director of Finance and Supplies Rivers State Ministry of Power. He had served as Permanent Secretary, Rivers State Ministry of Finance, Enviroment, Deputy Governor's office. He is currently the Permanent Secretary, Special Services, SSG' office, Rivers State.

H IGH CHIEF JEROME EKE

The ready smile, the generous nature, the friendly disposition and the gigantic figure, have for years been the most significant aspects of High Chief Jerome Eke. The years have been kind to his huge appearance which at an age that places him well over fifty, still retains the air of youthful exuberance. His mind has always been very alert and very quick. A conversation with this multi-millionaire enigma of progressive politics has all the attributes of a hard game of volley-ball: all the surprises demanding quick reflexes in a game, which is, at the same time, serious and hilarious, where the ball comes high over the net or just scraping it, and where the play is sometimes fast and sometimes slow. Whatever the tempo, a conversation with High Chief Jerome Eke always leaves an interlocutor breathless and at the end wondering why one had not said all that one would have wished to say. High Chief Jerome Eke always dominates conversations no matter the intellectual level of the person he talks with, no matter the person's education, the language or the erudition.

High Chief Jerome Eke is a veritable revolution all within himself. For as long as he can remember, he has been part of the struggle for Etche progress and for as long as anyone cares to remember, High Chief Jerome Eke has been part of the struggle to liberate Etche people. High Chief Eke is a great communicator, a mover of minds.

As a legislator in the National Assembly, High Chief Jerome Eke skillfully played himself into the mainstream. He was appointed Deputy chairman, House committee on industry. He was appointed member of the following House Committees; Petroleum(upstream), Rules and Business, and Education(UBEC).
Within six months of High Chief Jerome Eke's representation at the national assembly before the nullification of his election, he gave Etche people a sense of belonging at Abuja.

He has sponsored over six bills namely: Call for r e h a b i l i t a t i o n   o f

Igwuruta/Chokocho/Okehi/Igbodo/Okpala road; Call for rehabilitation of Rumukwurushi/Igbo/Chokocho/Ozuzu road; three Motion to retain one hundred and fifty-thousand naira (150,000) withdrawal limit for ATM and others.

He also co-sponsored the following motions:
1. Adverse effects of the absence of Nigeria at the Zero Routine Gas Flaring initiative in Washington D.C., USA
2. Call for enforcement of the Sea Fisheries Act in order to protect the Artisanal Fisherman.

HRH, EZE SIR KEN O. NWALA JP

The highly celebrated victory of the selection of HRH, Eze Sir Ken O. Nwala JP as the Onye-Ishi-Agwuru III Ulakwo-Umuselem Clan, began his coronation and reign in September 2014. His achievements this far as a king has proved that Eze Ken Nwala is built with extraordinary grace. He is a leader of great stature in every sense and eminently successful. He perceives his job as leading his people to greater heights with vigour and passion. Whenever he sees an opportunity for his people, he goes for it. He has dreams for his people and he is steadfast in the pursuit of that dream. He knows where he is going, and he is taking his people with him without deceit. He is loved by those he led, of both high and low estate. He understands the needs of his people and has continued to inspire them to heights which they never appeared to think possible.

On his return from service in 1993, he started work with Nigerian Bottling Company as a Special Event Officer and Photographer in 1994 and later joined Communication Trends Ltd as an Agents Supervisor 1996 and then proceeded to Multichioce (DSTV) Nigeria Ltd in 1997. In 1998, he started Corporate Communications Ltd and his company became a Dealer with Mtel Nigerian Communications Commission. On the inception of GSM telephony in Nigeria in 2001, the company became one of the pioneers of the service as a distributor to al the operators. He stepped up and incorporated Airpins System Ltd in 2010 as an IT service company. He is self motivated and a goal getter in everything he pursues.

PRINCESS ANN OPURUM

One beautiful Sunday morning, I chose to worship with a branch of Redeemed Christian Church of God located within D-line, Port Harcourt. During the two hours service, I observed with great interest a beautiful daughter of God seriously engaged as one of the officiating sang with the choir, stepped out to lead church during offering time, made announcement and she also served in the teen's church.

The joy and excitement with which she served in that church that very day can only be compared to Mary, the sister of Marta, who always ministered to our Lord, Jesus Christ. At the end of the service, tears of joy flowed freely through my eyes, at least we still have a Princess that loves the Lord and is graciously blessed with such amazing gifts of singing and leadership. I am referring to no other person than our own ebullient Princess Ann Enyinne Opurum, daughter of Onye-Ishi-Etche, His Eminence, Ochie ENB Opurum, MFR (JP).

Princess Annie as I fondly call her is a practical example to all young and adult females of Etche nation that beauty is not a gift for doing the wrongs things but is to serve the lord. She is a model and mentor to all the women who think that serving God is old fashioned. That is a lie from the pit of hell. Serving God is the most rewarding job anybody can engage in doing. This is because your reward is both here on earth and in heaven. I recommend absolute service and dependence on God as the sure strategy towards accomplishments in life. It is a guaranteed method to actualize destiny.

Her interest in becoming a great music minister is highly commendable. Christian Music is the food for human soul and spirit. God loves worship and praises. Whoever that is gifted with singing becomes Gods best friend, his right hand person, cause singers sit at the right hand of God in heaven.

We should all be proud of her. When she becomes a great music minister in the coming years, we would have gotten another Etche Ambassador of repute.

CHAPTER TWENTY-ONE

CONCLUSION:
RANDOM REFLECTIONS

Today, we are still a long way from our desired goal which is to achieve for Etche people, respect among the comity of Nationalities in Nigeria.

The struggle for the restoration of our dignity can only be a continuing one. It is incumbent on Etche people to find solutions to our predicament in the context of the Nigerian nation.

On Etche unity

Our very survival is through unity. Without unity we shall perish. We must be prepared to approach the issue of unity and local solidarity realistically, selflessly, fearlessly and with a singularity of purpose. We must over come old prejudices and entrenched interest. We must banish for every Etche person the atmosphere of insecurity.

Politics and The Etches

Democracy has come to stay in Nigeria. It is a game for the optimists and socialites. There is no place in politics for the pessimist. Politics is a game of chance played by the optimist. Difficulties are mere obstacles placed in the field which only men may remove. Politics is a science of leverage and leverage depends on numbers. Therefore, one cannot expect much from politics if one does not have the requisite numbers.

The Etche people must advance into the mainstream of Nigerian politics. Isolationism and wallowing in an orgy of self-pity or indeed carrying the banner of protest is counter productive. If we persist in complaining, weeping and wailing and bemoaning our fate, we risk the bitter sweet test of drowning in the brackish water of our tears.

The Etche people must face the future with full courage which our Nigeria citizenship bestows upon us. We must move forward with optimism and ignore the doomsday ratings of some of our brothers.

The Issue of Leadership

One essential demand of leadership is to be like a waste - paper basket, a dustbin where all dirt and rubbish are heaped. Whoever is not ready to accept such treatment does not qualify to be a leader. A leader must be prepared to tolerate the excesses of people.

Every leader must have dream and be steadfast in his efforts to fulfill that dream. Service to a people is not a profession. It is a vocation and a leader must make sacrifices for it. A leader does not complain when things are not going too well since that is one of the occupational hazards. A leader must not try to cushion himself (by amassing wealth) against the future. Though the temptation is great, there is nothing more counter productive in leadership than corruption. A leader, apart. from constantly reassuring his people, must always make himself acceptable to every-one. To do this, he has to be above board in his dealings.

On the need for education
Education is the process of moulding individuals in the society in order to develop their natural potentials and become engines of growth. Education is transformation. It cultures and reforms the individual for the better. It affords the individual the opportunity to be fit and balanced mentally, economically, politically and morally to tackle the environmental challenges posed to him. The education level of a society has a lot to do with the level of educational development of members of such a society. In the words of Francis Bacon, 'knowledge is power". Education is the gateway to empowerment. Education arises out of the need to solve problems.

Political followership

Political followership in Etche, is to say the least, extremely supine. Followership has become such that our leaders are seduced and tyrants made out of them. We are sycophants. We are very docile people. We genuflect to mediocrity and defend the indefensible executive indiscretions.

On Rivers State

In its almost forty years of creation, Rivers State has been through several critical times. We have even gone through military rule. But at present, we are going through difficulties brought about by our fresh experiment in democratic governance. In order to realize and manifest our destiny as a people, we need to enthrone a leadership that is anchored on the fear of God and sincerity of purpose. Since the return of democracy in 1999, Ex-Governor Peter Odili and Governor Chibuike Amaechi have done their best to stabilize the ship of the state and move Rivers State forward but there is need to devise a solid, all-round developmental strategy through which their achievements can be consolidated. It is incontestable that Rivers State is blessed by God as the treasure base of the Nigeria. With rich human and natural resources, the State should ordinarily be occupying a pride of place among the comity of states. But that is not the case. Rather, we have seen states without similar potentials doing better than us. What this means is that we have failed to get the most critical factor right.

Injustice & Justice

There are glaring cases of injustice in all spheres of life in Nigeria. There is the injustice of people trained but have no jobs, injustice in our access to serving he country, injustice in the sharing of national responsibility and assets, religions and ethnic injustice, as well as injustice lodged in the fact that salaries do not reflect work, nor wages, the labour put in. There is injustice meted to my people -The Etches. The time for political justice is now.

It would be difficult to achieve justice in Nigeria because of our perception of the true meaning of justice. Nigeria's perception of justice is definitely not in line with the 'us all' concept, but rather it is to be found in the context of 'us' and 'them' dichotomy. Anything goes for those who belong to 'us'. Our perception of justice is influenced by our territorial imperative and not until we accept the 'us all' concept can there be any from of social justice.

On Forgiveness

Human nature is such that one remembers only that which is convenient. The duration of our memory of any wrong-doing directly reflects our capacity to maintain our individuality. Nigerians tend to forget hatred easily because they have to reconcile themselves with life. The same applies to Etche people. If one finds oneself totally emasculated by circumstance, what one does is to find a convenient way of continuing ones existence. To say that Nigerians, albeit Etche people, have short memories will be a bit too patronizing. They remember only that which is convenient for them to remember and forget the others.

On Violence

I call for an end to violence of all types in Etche land. I urge my people to seek peace through dialogue. Having studied the history of the civil war in Nigeria, the most crucial lesson I discovered is that no dispute, however, seemingly intractable, can defy dialogue and a genuine search for a meeting of minds.

On Ogbako Etche Socio-Cultural Organisation

Our political system in Etcheland should be revitalized by the resuscitation of the Etche Socio-cultural organization - Ogbako Etche. And that union should play its role as a check on the excesses of politicians who may wish to substitute their personal ambition for the interest of all Etche people in a unified and prosperous Nigeria.

On Etche Heritage Foundation(EHF)

Among several noticeable socio-political groups in Etche, Etche Heritage Foundation(EHF) is the only one I accepted to be a member. Its vision is sharp, its mission is action-oriented and its goals are achievable. However, the group knowingly or unknowingly allowed elements of politics to infiltrate and weaken its structure. The Foundation's foundation has unconsciously been tampered. If EHF is to fly again, its foundation has to be properly redesigned and reconstructed without bias, fear or compromise. Without such moves, EHF may be dead and buried.

On Ogbako Etche Action Group

The formation of Ogbako Etche Action Group by the leadership of Ogbako Etche Socio-Cultural Organization and its Grand Patron, Eze E.N.B Opurum, Onye-Ishi-Etche is a wise move in the right direction. I believe the major purpose for such action is to strengthen the Ogbako Etche Socio-Cultural Organization by appointing eminent sons and daughters of Etche to chart a new course for Etche nation were necessary. We hope that the group , eminently chaired by HRH Eze Sir Ken Nwala JP, Onye-Ishi-Agwuru Ulakwo/Umuselem Clan, deputized by Captain Sunday Nwankwo, and with my humble self - David Oguzierem as the Secretary will not disappoint Etche people to this regard.

Afterword

The advancement of any nation begins with the development of the individuals that make up that nation; which in itself is the outcome of the extent of awareness and enlightenment of the minds of the people. It is the level of education and understanding of the situation, resources and needs of the place and the response of the leading group, in tackling the needs that bring about transformation; be it spiritual, economic, social, infrastructural or political. That is why, no one with the desire for change can undermine the relevance of this book which seeks to awaken, as it were, the sleeping giant and to set the path in sensitizing Etche leaders to rise up to the challenge of defending the trust which their positions place on them.

Oscar S. Strauss once said. *"There is a higher form of Patrotism than nationalism, and that higher form is not limited by the boundaries of one's*

country, but by a duty to mankind, to safeguard the trust of civilization".

One is not educated, patriotic or elitist, if his knowledge or virtue is only useful to himself. David has unburdened his heart and shared the vision of his dream Etche. He has shown that to be educated is to pledge to impact on the land and society, without which education is useless.

Reading through this book pulls a trigger in the minds of those of us who are passionate about the restoration of the dignity of the Etche man, placing the nation where it ought to be. '

The author opens the eyes of his audience to why we are not yet in our pride of place. He identifies the reasons for the situation as lack of early education, tribal and political disunity, the gap in the political evolution of Etche, and manpower shortage. Also, most of the early workforce took to teaching; other causes include but not limited to godlessness, communal crisis, and idleness, too much food to the point of wastage, and chieftaincy tussle.

Idleness is a waste of time and resources. In fact, it is very costly to be idle. Though there is no profit from idleness, one is compelled to spend money for the consumption of the things he wouldn't have had time to, were he busy at work. That is why some idle persons take to crime. Sometimes to make money in order to solve the problem created either by lack of job or their refusal to work.   .

The effect ascendance to chieftaincy stools through squabbling, backstabbing, malicious mischief, blackmail and violence has on the land throughout the lifetime of the said traditional ruler and beyond is devastating. It is a throne built on blood, and masterminded by evil powers whose outcome is unsafe.

Reading through this motivational, thought provoking and revolutionary piece, reveals the giant strides Etche has made in politics earlier than many other ethnic groups in Nigeria. Which should have well positioned her on the threshold of development such that (if there was continuity), Etche should have been boasting as one of the leading political entities in the present Nigeria. It chronicles the political development of Etche from pre-independence era and how Etche sons played prominent roles in the success of the popular National Council of Nigeria and the Cameroons (NCNC) and worked with Dr. Nnamdi Azikiwe and other leading African nationalists. A nation that had political heavy weights, who bargained and achieved political autonomy by the creation of the Etche county council in the early 1950s. During the very first federal democratic elections in Nigeria, a key player in the then Etche politics, Chief J .H.E. Nwuke was elected into the Eastern Regional assembly and afterwards appointed as a regional minister into the Eastern Regional executive council with Chief Johan Akor elected into the Federal House of Representatives representing Ahoada

North/East federal constituency. Without going further to reflect one of the most detailed political history of Etche which the author has painstakingly put down, one big question is ***"how has Etche fallen from that position of a political giant to now political beggar"?***

Politics, Development & Minorities In Nigeria was written with the right pen. The aspiring great author writes with the mastery of circular history, politics and not just religion but Christianity. The reference to the Holy Bible, in the gospel according to St. Luke chapter 4: 1719 is very remarkable. *(The scroll of the prophet Isaiah was handed to him. Unrolling it, he found the place .where it is written; "the spirit of the Lord is on me because he has anointed me to preach go news to the poor. He has sent me to proclaim freedom to the prisoners, and recovery of sight for the blind, to release the oppressed and to proclaim the year of Lord's favour.)* For those who understand the purpose of Christ's mission, it is referred to as *"the Christological manifesto;* it sums up what Jesus came to do, that is "to liberate man from the slavery of sin, poverty, disease and death". At the end of the reading of that prophecy, which marked the official declaration of Jesus ministry, the Lord said in the 21st verse, ***"today, this scripture is fulfilled before your eyes"*** that means, that the time of freedom for humanity which had been foretold ages before had been accomplished by His incarnation. How many elites of Etche understand the purpose of their birth and the power their exposure to western education gives to them? Living in rebellion against the purpose of God describes why people could be suffering in the midst of huge natural, human and material resources which God has provided for man to make living meaningful.

When people reject God, his creation becomes opposed to the good of man. It was after the fall of man, that the same earth which God had said he should subdue became rebellious against him to the point of producing thistles that make man's labour on earth painful. That man's original place of authority and freedom is what Jesus came to restore. The significance of this reference to the work therefore foreshadows the liberation of Etche. Today, change, hope and freedom are proclaimed over Etche land.

Blacks in America and other nations today are reaping the fruits of struggles by several black leaders like Malcolm X, Martin Luther King Jnr and others who severally championed the movement for black liberation in seeking to secure progress on civil rights for blacks in the United States. It may have taken time and faced several oppositions, civil and mortal, but today, there is an air of freedom for black Americans. The emergence of Barak Obama as the first America black president crowns it all.

Worthy of note is that Martin Luther King Jnr, was inspired through the work of Ghandhi (1869-1948); Indian's nationalist and reform leader who was a key figure in the campaign and negotiation for independence with Britain.

Information is power, which is why all those who crave for the growth of Etche land need to make this book their companion. There cannot be liberty unless people pay the prize. One of the greatest problems of Etche is not the marginalization and setback we are crying against, but lack of the will by the enlightened class to pay the prize for the future of our people. Not many people are concerned. Some who claim to be do not commit themselves to the extent of risking their time, lives and resources.

The author has paid a prize for liberty by revealing the secrets of the underdevelopment of the Etche land, and suggested ways through which the nation could be pulled out of the veil of backwardness. According to G.B. Shaw, ***"liberty means responsibility. That is why most men dread it".*** Not many people will dare to write as bluntly as the author has done, but except a people are free, struggles, agitations and violence cannot cease. R.G Ingersoll speaking on the same subject said, ***"What light is to the eyes, what air is to the lungs, what love is to the heart, liberty is to the soul of man ".*** There is no rest, nor fulfillment to the man who has been denied freedom and access to the necessary amenities that make daily living worthwhile.

If change could be achieved just by putting ink on the paper, then this book would have been enough to solve the Etche problem. As soul searching as it is, our earnest prayer is that it penetrates into the right ears. Those who do not want to eat only now, but use the privileges of today to secure a future for posterity.

In memory of those who championed the course for political and educational advancement of the Etche nation; to those who desire to leave their comfort zones to contribute towards the realization of a greater Etche. And to those of other nations who want to be great and need to know the secrets of great men and nations of history. To the glory of God Almighty and the manifestation of the saving grace of the Lord Jesus Christ upon the Etche nation, this book is graciously commended.

The Rt. Revd. Okechukwu Precious Nwala
(Justice of the Peace)
Bishop of Etche, Anglican Communion.

APPENDIX I

NEXT ETCHE
DEVELOPMENT PROJECT

3rd June 2015

His Excellency, General Muhammadu Buhari,
President of the Federal Republic of Nigeria,
Aso villa,
Abuja.

A PEOPLE WHOSE FATE IN NIGERIA IS UNKNOWN

1. Your Excellency, we write to officially congratulate you on your successful emergence and swearing-in as the President and Commander-in-Chief of the federal republic of Nigeria. Our prayer is that Almighty God will guide you as you lead Nigeria to greater heights.

2. Your Excellency, we are NEXT ETCHE DEVELOPMENT PROJECT(NEDEP) a foremost socio-political organization of Etche people in Rivers State. Our major aim is to champion the integration, empowerment, promotion and protection of Etche people and their inalienable rights and interest in Nigeria.

3. Your Excellency, we write to draw your attention to the stagnation and marginalization of Etche people which is unjust and unfair.

4. Your Excellency, Etche is one of the largest ethnic

nationalities in Rivers State. It has two Local Government Areas of 29 wards, three House of assembly constituencies and one federal constituency. During the colonial era, the leaders of Etche played important roles in old Port Harcourt province which today is the present Rivers State. Chief J.H.E. Nwuke was the first Provincial Commissioner in the old Port Harcourt Province. He was a minister in the former Eastern Region. Chief Akor was a member of Federal House of representative, representing both Ikwerre and Etche Federal constituencies.

5. Your Excellency, during the agitation for state creation of Rivers State, one of our illustrious sons, His Eminence, Ochie Emmanuel Opurum MFR, JP, in company of Chief Dappa Biriye of blessed memory, from Bonny Kingdom championed the fight for the creation of Rivers state. Thus, Etche made a lot of impact in the socio-political and economic emancipation of the present Niger Delta.

6. Your Excellency, in the economic sector, Etche Ethnic Nationality has contributed trillions of dollars to the coffers of Nigerian Government through prolonged uninterrupted oil and gas exploitation since 1958. The Bonny light crude oil which is internationally highly priced is produced from Umuechem oil fields in Etche. Apart from Umuechem oil exploration, other towns

such as Odagwa, Egwi, Okereagu, Isu, Akpoku, Abara, Ikwerre Ngwo, Umuakali, Umuebulu, Ozuzu among others, are Shell oil locations.

7. Your Excellency, beside oil exploitation, Etche donated most of its agricultural lands to the government of Rivers State. The Rubber Estates at Odagwa, Umuanyagu, Abara, Umuoye and Akpoku; the Risonpalm plantation at Ozuzu, Isu, Ogida, Ihie, Egbu and the School-to-land project sited at Egbeke and Nwuba are all in Etche. All these agricultural plantations are today lying fallow and have not in any way impacted positively on Etche people. The Risonpalm which is supposed to create employment to its landlords is not doing much. Presently the rest of the agricultural lands at Obibi, Akwa, Odagwa, Ulakwo and Okereagu are now being acquired by the present Rivers State government. Very soon Etche will not have a place to farm.

8. Your Excellency, the NDDC and Ministry of Niger Delta which is established to develop oil producing areas of Niger Delta has never had any Etche indigene as executive director or senior management staff in the establishment. Most of the projects carried out by NDDC in Etcheland are either done shoddily or abandoned. The irony of it all is that there is no good road leading to Etche from the state capital. Consequently it is difficult for Etche people to go home.

9. Your Excellency, the role of Shell Petroleum

Development Company (SPDC) which is an oil and gas exploration company in Etche has brought untold hardship to the host communities. For instance, the November 1ˢᵗ 1990 Massacre in Umuechem community, which claimed the life of a government recognized traditional ruler, HRH Eze A. A Ordu and others. Odagwa crisis that led to the killing of people, among others are examples of shell's atrocities in Etcheland. Shell has totally neglected their corporate social responsibilities to the host communities in total disregard to the MOU and other agreements reached with them.

10. Your Excellency, there was genocide committed against Etche people during the Nigeria/Biafra civil war and the genocide committed by SHELL in Umuchem in Etche LGA in Nov 1990. While there is a conscious effort to settle the people of Ogoni and the people of Odi, there is a deliberate effort to suppress the Etche incident.

11. Your Excellency, Etche ethnic nationality is the only autonomous ethnicity that was not allowed to participate in the 2013 constitutional conference conducted by former President Goodluck Jonathan.

Therefore we make the following demands:

1. That Etche by virtue of her contribution to the economy of the state (arguably the second largest

producer of oil and gas with 250 producing oil wells), Etche by virtue of her large population (1.2 million) and landmass (1300 square km, the second largest in the state) and Etche by virtue of her comparably teeming large manpower base (doctors, engineers, lawyers, accountants, managers, politicians, with a significant number in the Diaspora) must and should imperatively be considered in the forefront of this current political rumble.

2. That in the post election slates, Etche should be appointed to different political positions such as ministers, ambassadors, presidential advisers, Chairman of federal agencies, and Director-General of federal agency, and allocation of oil block license.

3. That in view of the present security challenges in Etche, we call on the state and federal governments, relevant security agencies, to urgently intervene in the security situation in Etcheland to ensure that peace reigns.

4. That the above mentioned demands should be urgently addressed through Ogbako Etche and Etche Supreme Council of Traditional Rulers and Chiefs to avoid the breakdown of law and order by the youths who are itching to take laws into their hands by

shutting down all the operational Oil wells in Etcheland.

Your Excellency, we assure your government of our continuous total support and commitment.

Sincerely,

David .E. Oguzierem
Coordinator, NEDEP

APPENDIX II

OGBAKO ETCHE
A C T I O N G R O U P

23rd Dec. 2015

His Excellency,
Chief Ezenwo Nyesom Wike, CON
Governor of Rivers State

<u>OPEN LETTER TO THE EXECUTIVE GOVERNOR OF RIVERS
STATE HIS EXCELLENCY, BARR. NYESOM EZENWO WIKE</u>

Your Excellency, the good people of Etche appreciates your achievements since assumption of office as Executive Governor of Rivers State.

We the OGBAKO ETCHE ACTION GROUP write to draw your attention to the unfair treatment of Etche people in the scheme of affairs in Rivers State and Nigeria at large. Etche as a distinct ethnic nationality of Etche and Omuma local government areas is currently in the Rivers East Senatorial District.

Your Excellency, it will interest you to know that since the return of democratic government in 1999, apart from the usual statutory positions of every LGA which includes House of Representatives, House of Assembly, Chairman of Local Government and Commissioners, there has not been any Etche person who has occupied such higher positions such as the SSG, Chief of Staff, Speaker of the

House of Assembly and other key appointments in the state. At the federal level, Etche has been omitted from all key positions such as Senator, Minister, Ambassador, Presidential Advisor, DG, Permanent Secretaries, Executive Secretaries and Chairmen of MDG's.

A quick enumeration here will suffice to highlight the gross absence of Etche from high political equation: Ijaws have produced two (civilian) Governors, numerous ministers, Senators, Presidential Advisers, Heads of Parastatals, SSGs, Speakers of the Houses of Assembly, Ambassadors, etc. Ogonis have produced many Senators, SSGs, Ministers, Presidential Advisers, etc. The Ndonis and Ogbas have produced a Governor, Senators and Ministers; Ikwerres have produced Governors, Ministers, Senators, Speaker, Ambassadors, and Deputy Speaker of the House of Representative etc.

In the current political dispensation, we foresee a similar trend which is worrisome and which Etche people cannot continue to ignore.

Etche people have contributed immensely to the overall development of Rivers State. For instance, during the struggle for the creation of Rivers State, a prominent son of Etche, HRM Eze ENB Opurum MFR fought assiduously alongside Late Chief Harold Dappa prieye and few others to actualize our state creation. Etche remains the second largest producer of oil and gas with over 250 producing oil wells. We are third largest Ethnic group in the state with a population of over 1.4 million and a landmass of about 1300 square km and the second largest in the state. Our manpower base comprises of all professionals which includes eminent Professors, experienced Doctors, Engineers, Lawyers, Accountants, Managers, Politicians, etc within the country and in Diaspora.

Your Excellency, in NDDC and Ministry of Niger Delta which are established by law to develop oil producing areas of which ETCHELAND is a major contributor, no Etche indigene has EVER held any position of Managing Director, Executive Director and Rivers State Reps in the boards. Ironically the roads leading to the oil producing communities in Etche are in very serious deplorable conditions. These roads include IgwurutaChokocho-Okehi-Okpala Road, Rumukrushi-Igbo-Umuchem-Ozuzu-Owerri Road, Igwuruta-Umuchem-Egwi Road, Ulakwo-Odagwa-Omuma road, Oyibo-Umuebule-Igbo road, Umuebule internal roads, Umuanyagu-Okeroagu-Odagwa-Akwa roads.

OUR PASSIONATE APPEAL
Your Excellency, Etche people passionately appeal for Government quick rehabilitation and reconstruction of these two exit roads namely Igwuruta-Chokocho-Okehi-Igbodo roads and Rumukrushi-Igbo-Umuchem-Ozuzu

roads to enable our people easy access within this yuletide season.

Your Excellency, we also appeal for your kind consideration in the appointment of our sons and daughters into key positions in your government as we ask for your recommendation of our people for federal appointments.

We also appeal that Etche should be included in all your developmental agenda for Rivers State especially the ongoing renovation of Government Schools.

Please be assured of our continued support and best wishes for your government.

Yours Truly,

HRH Eze K. O. Nwala KSC JP.   Mr. David E. Oguzierem
Chairman, OEAG   Secretary, OEAG
(Onye Ishi Agwuru III Ulakwo/Umuselem clan)

www.ingramcontent.com/pod-product-compliance
Lightning Source LLC
Chambersburg PA
CBHW072037280526
45788CB00006B/2103